PRAISE FOR *JOY BOMB*

I've always been intentional about living with joy—on and off the court. But little did I know, my definition of joy may have been too shallow, confined to just a feeling and a smile. In *Joy Bomb*, Tauren Wells delivers an electrifying message about the power of true joy—one that isn't fleeting or dependent on circumstances, but deeply rooted in faith. This book is a must-read for anyone seeking to reclaim joy, break free from the pressures of the world, and embrace the abundant life God has promised.

—STEPHEN CURRY, PROFESSIONAL BASKETBALL PLAYER;
FOUR-TIME NBA CHAMPION

We all go through disappointments, and it's easy to get discouraged and let the pressures of life weigh us down. We must remember that our joy is a necessity, directly connected to the strength we need to overcome our difficulties. The enemy does not come for your dreams, your children, your health, or your finances; he comes first for your joy. If he can steal that, he knows you won't have the strength to protect the other things. When you get up in the morning, you must set your mind on being joyful and declare that God is on the throne and is fighting your battles. When you understand and accept that God is for you, that he is greater than everything in the world coming against you, you can preserve your joy, and you cannot be defeated.

This principle is well illustrated in my friend Tauren Wells's new book, *Joy Bomb*. Tauren is a well-known and highly respected minister, impacting millions of people in nations throughout the world. His message contained in this book is one of purpose, restoration, strength, and victory, all found when you draw upon the joy of the Lord. I encourage you to let these words help you overcome the troubles of this world and discover the triumphant life God created you to have.

—JOEL OSTEEN, #1 *NEW YORK TIMES* BESTSELLING AUTHOR;
COPASTOR, LAKEWOOD CHURCH

Tauren Wells is a tank-filler! Whether in a song or a sermon, in singing or speaking, he has my attention. Tauren has this unique ability of delivering what I call "platinum nuggets" (better than gold) that I immediately tuck away in my heart and ponder on for quite some time. I'll never forget having a conversation with Tauren when I was walking through one of my hardest professional seasons. Unknowingly, he summarized in one statement what I had been trying to figure out for months! He gave me divine direction that day, and it was the pivot I needed to see what the Lord was doing.

Tauren does much the same thing in this book. His words take the Beatitudes of Jesus straight to the heart. As you read, you'll experience moments like I had in conversation with Tauren that pivotal day—"platinum nuggets" that are filled with the power of the Spirit so your life can be filled with joy. *Joy Bomb* isn't just the name of the book—it's the experience you'll have as you open your heart and let Jesus's explosive teaching fill your tank and direct your life.

—CARMEN BROWN, THE JOY FM

Tauren Wells is a powerful example of what it means to represent God with excellence, authenticity, and joy. His life and music radiate the kind of joy that can only come from a deep, unwavering faith in Christ. Whether on stage or in everyday moments, he puts Christ at the center of culture, reminding us all that worship isn't just a sound—it's a lifestyle. And this book will be no different. It will challenge, inspire, and equip you to live with purpose and passion!

—MICHAEL TODD, #1 *NEW YORK TIMES* BESTSELLING AUTHOR;
LEAD PASTOR, TRANSFORMATION CHURCH

Joy Bomb is more than a book about joy—it's an invitation to see joy through the lens of Jesus. Anchored in the profound truths of the Sermon on the Mount, this book unpacks how happiness flows from a life deeply rooted in him. Prepare to be inspired, challenged, and forever changed by the joy Jesus offers.

—DR. DHARIUS DANIELS, AUTHOR, *RELATIONAL INTELLIGENCE*

Joy Bomb is a powerful and timely reminder of the profound joy found in Jesus's teachings. With his trademark clarity and heart, Tauren unpacks the Beatitudes in a way that detonates hope and happiness in the soul. This book will inspire you to live with deeper purpose and extraordinary joy.

—DEREK CARR, NFL QUARTERBACK

What a perfect book for Tauren to write. Tauren spreads "joy in the morning" and the *Joy Bomb* wherever he goes. Jesus spoke about joy throughout his life and wants us to experience this wonderful gift. This book is a blessed reminder that true joy can only be found in the Lord.

—DEBRA WALLER, CEO, JOCKEY INTERNATIONAL

Joy Bomb is a game changer for anyone longing to experience the fullness of joy. This book is not just a read—it's an invitation to a transformed life. With deep biblical insights and personal reflections, Tauren masterfully unpacks the Beatitudes, revealing that joy isn't found in your circumstances but in the unshakable truth of who God is. Whether you're navigating life's valleys or standing on its peaks, *Joy Bomb* will equip you with the spiritual tools to cultivate a joy that cannot be stolen. If you desire a life marked by divine happiness, hope, and strength, this book is your guide. It's time to detonate the joy bomb and step into the extraordinary life God has prepared for you!

—CLINT PHILLIPS, CEO, MEDICI

Tauren Wells has done something very special with *Joy Bomb*—he's taken a subject that many of us assume we already understand and shown us that there's so much more to joy and happiness than we ever thought. Whether you're in a difficult season or, like so many of us, have a sense that there's more for you, this book will show you the way to the source of true contentment and how to hold on to it.

—BRAD O'DONNELL, PRESIDENT,
CAPITOL CHRISTIAN MUSIC GROUP

I first met Tauren Wells when he was just twelve years old, and even then, his joy was undeniable. Whether he is preaching, singing, or writing, that joy has only grown over the years—but it has never changed. In this book, Tauren combines humor, storytelling, and God's Word to teach kingdom principles that will help you detonate the *Joy Bomb* in your own life.

—REV. DAVID MOREHEAD, CAMPUS PASTOR,
THE CALVARY ACADEMY

"The joy of the Lord is your strength." These powerful words, spoken by Nehemiah, the religious reformer, reminded a broken people—grieving their past while rebuilding a fallen Jerusalem—that their strength was not in their failures but in God's grace and presence.

This is the heart of *Joy Bomb*, a book that ignites an internal explosion of joy when you realize that "The Greater One" lives in you! Tauren Wells masterfully weaves biblical truth with personal insight, showing that joy isn't circumstantial—it's supernatural. If you're ready to live with unshakable strength and breakthrough joy, this book is your invitation to a life-changing encounter with the source of all joy—Jesus!

—A. R. BERNARD, AUTHOR; PRESIDENT/CEO, A. R. MEDIA

I've been cheering Tauren on for years in all of his adventures, and *Joy Bomb* is no exception. This book shines a light on joy in the Bible while offering new perspectives. Readers, get ready for a journey of understanding Jesus as the ultimate detonator of our "Joy Bombs"—get to know him, get to know joy! I can't wait to see the positive impact *Joy Bomb* will make for the kingdom.

—SADIE ROBERTSON HUFF, AUTHOR;
SPEAKER; FOUNDER, LIVE ORIGINAL

JOY BOMB

Unleash Jesus's Explosive Joy
for an Extraordinary Life

TAUREN WELLS

ZONDERVAN
BOOKS

ZONDERVAN BOOKS

Joy Bomb
Copyright © 2025 by Tauren Wells

Published in Grand Rapids, Michigan, by Zondervan. Zondervan is a registered trademark of The Zondervan Corporation, L.L.C., a wholly owned subsidiary of HarperCollins Christian Publishing, Inc.

Requests for information should be addressed to customercare@harpercollins.com.

Zondervan titles may be purchased in bulk for educational, business, fundraising, or sales promotional use. For information, please email SpecialMarkets@Zondervan.com.

ISBN 978-0-310-36894-6 (audio)

Library of Congress Cataloging-in-Publication Data

Names: Wells, Tauren, 1986- author.
Title: Joy bomb : unleash Jesus's explosive joy for an extraordinary life / Tauren Wells.
Description: Grand Rapids, Michigan : Zondervan Books, [2025]
Identifiers: LCCN 2024060645 (print) | LCCN 2024060646 (ebook) | ISBN 9780310368908
    (hardcover) | ISBN 9780310368922 (ebook)
Subjects: LCSH: Joy--Religious aspects--Christianity. | Christian life. | BISAC: RELIGION /
    Christian Living / Inspirational | RELIGION / Christian Living / Personal Growth
Classification: LCC BV4647.J68 W455 2025 (print) | LCC BV4647.J68 (ebook) | DDC
    248.4--dc23/eng/20250216
LC record available at https://lccn.loc.gov/2024060645
LC ebook record available at https://lccn.loc.gov/2024060646

Cover design: Aaron Stearns
Cover photo: Hannah Corwin
Interior design: Sara Colley

Printed in the United States of America

25 26 27 28 29 LBC 5 4 3 2 1

To Jesus, who has done more with my
life than I ever thought possible.
To Lorna, Kanaan, Lawson, Navy, Banner—
I have something very important to tell you . . .

CONTENTS

FOREWORD

When Tauren asked me to write the foreword for his book on joy, it took me a little while to decide whether I could do it. Not because I don't believe in the message, and certainly not because I don't believe in his ability to deliver it. Anyone who has ever encountered the melody and the ministry of Tauren Wells knows how contagious his spirit is. (And if you haven't caught it yet, you will in the pages ahead.)

My hesitation to write this foreword was more about a feeling of my own hypocrisy. Let me explain. A few summers ago, I had taken my wife and three kids on vacation, and one day over lunch I decided to play a conversational game. "Who's the happiest person you know?" I asked. I started by casting my vote for my wife, Holly. I thought maybe she'd reciprocate by naming me when it was her turn. No chance. Nobody in the family nominated me. I don't even think I was in their top ten, honestly.

So you understand now why, when Tauren told me he had written *Joy Bomb* and wanted my voice to introduce the message, I had to pause. I don't exactly feel like most days my attitude is the best endorsement of joy. Even as I was writing this while sitting at my son's wrestling match, a coach walked over to me and said, "You look very stressed. What are you working on?"

A foreword for my happy friend's book about joy, if you can believe that.

So I am here not only as someone who recommends this book to you but as someone who needs it himself. I need it for my down days, my frequent funks, and the—what shall we call them?—"attitudinal challenges" that I battle daily.

I need a voice to remind me to dig beneath the surface of what the world calls happiness and tap into the "Wells" of joy that God alone can open.

And I don't think there's a better friend than Tauren to explain the nature and habits of sustainable joy that comes straight from the source.

As you'll see, this isn't "seven hacks to have a good day," although this book is loaded with practical application. This is timeless truth of what it means to live in the flow of God's supply instead of in the state of stress and scarcity that comes from self-absorption.

There are very few preachers, singers, and people who can instantly lift an entire room like Tauren does. But his vocal ability and spiritual vocabulary are only a part of his gift. The words he speaks emerge from the life he lives. He has done what one songwriter called "the hard work of happiness." In other words, he's dug deep.

And now he wants to help you do the same.

You're holding a bomb in your hand. The message God has given my friend has the power to destroy strongholds of depression, fear, and shame.

But you're also holding a balm in your hand. This message will be healing medicine for the wounds of your disappointments, and a shot of strength to your weary soul.

I invite you to join me on this journey called joy.

I've got a long way to go. But I can't think of a better guide.

STEVEN FURTICK

INTRODUCTION

Your joy is under attack.

I know that's not the most encouraging way to start a book you picked up for a dose of encouragement! But hang in there; there's plenty of good stuff coming. We just need to start with a reality check: Invisible forces are trying to mess with your happiness and drain your strength. But of course you know this already.

I don't need to throw a bunch of statistics at you. I could— about the rising rates of depression and anxiety, about the growing number of young people who say that they have no purpose or meaning in their lives, or about the number of people reporting serious mental health struggles. But do we really need the numbers? No. In fact, I'm sure you could tell *me* something about all of this.

Life can be brutal sometimes. We all have moments when it feels as though everything that can go wrong does go wrong. The loss of a loved one, a breakup, a dream that didn't pan out—the hits keep coming. Each one chips away at our resilience, making it tougher to find joy in the chaos. And it's not just the big stuff. The wear and tear of the daily grind has its own challenges. But whether our lives have been easy or we've been through unimaginably hard things, the problem we all face is the same—sometimes *the joy is gone.*

That's why I wrote this book. It's a reminder that even when we hit rock bottom, there's something deeper. Beneath the frozen ground of our tough situations, there's a fresh, powerful current of God's goodness and grace, creating a joy that we can't find on our own.

We often think of joy as something fleeting, a momentary high that comes and goes. We chase after it, thinking the next vacation, promotion, or purchase will make us happy. But joy isn't a passing feeling tied to what happens around us. It's not just a temporary thing that fades. Joy is much deeper and more profound. It's a state of being that can sustain us even in the darkest times.

We were made for joy. We were made for happiness that isn't tied to our next vacation, glass of wine, or new gadget. It's not even about God making all our dreams come true. Our joy is connected to one singular source. The kind of joy we're talking about here isn't superficial or dependent on circumstances; it's divine and eternal. It comes from God and is rooted in his unchanging character and boundless love for us.

The Bible says that the joy of the Lord is our strength (Nehemiah 8:10). I've found this to be true. When the Enemy targets my strength, he aims to sabotage my joy, because my strength flows from my joy. So if my strength is powered by my joy, I must ask: What is my joy connected to?

*

Many of us grapple with the elusive sensation of joy in our lives because we often tether our joy to fleeting and fragile sources. Our spirits will always feel drained when our joy is anchored to something momentary. Imagine if our joy is rooted in a job promotion and then we're passed over—suddenly our spirit feels crushed and our strength depleted. If our joy is wrapped up in another person and that person leaves our life for any reason, our joy goes with them, leaving us hollow. When our joy hinges on the next big achievement and we fall short, our joy perishes alongside our unmet goals. But when our joy is linked to its true and eternal source, a divine conduit designed to perpetuate an endless flow, we can sustain the current of God's power in our lives, even through any season and every storm!

We must recognize that our joy is meant to flow from a single unshakable source, and that source is the Lord. When our joy is intertwined with Jesus, it becomes impervious to the Enemy's assaults, because the Enemy must confront Jesus to even touch our joy! That's why it's crucial to remain in Christ, our supernatural source.

Are you ready for an infusion of encouragement? When you allow the joy of Jesus to surge through you, he imparts the strength you need to navigate whatever challenge you're facing right now and at any point in the future!

I know this is a book, but I feel compelled to preach a little bit! Jesus can infuse you with the strength required, by the joy he gives, to overcome any trial. One of my heroes, Pastor Steven Furtick, called me on the phone one night to talk through a message he was about to preach the next morning. I was preparing to walk out on stage for a concert, but I had to take a praise break in my dressing room when he pointed out that David proclaimed, "Yea, though I walk through the valley of the shadow of death, I will fear no evil" (Psalm 23:4 NKJV). He alluded to the idea that the joy of the Lord transforms your journey through the darkest night into a triumphant procession, allowing you to exclaim "Yea!" even when you're in the valley. Come on, that's good! He's right. This divine joy doesn't diminish the reality of your pain or the gravity of your struggles; rather, it grants you a steadfast spirit and unwavering confidence, ensuring that as you journey through trials, you are indeed moving through them. There is another side to every valley, and you are going to reach it!

Something caught my attention as I recently read through the Old Testament's last book, Malachi. The prophet concludes his writing with the word "curse" (4:6 NKJV). The story of God and his people doesn't exactly end on a high note, I'd say. But it was fitting because in their inability to uphold God's law, the laws of Moses, and their own stringent traditions, they were left with nothing but a curse. The people of Israel had been given a divine standard to live by, but their repeated failures highlighted their human frailty and the insurmountable gap between divine perfection and human imperfection. This is where the connections in Scripture find their place and power. As Jesus, God in flesh, began his ministry on earth, as captured in the pages of what we call the New Testament, he opened his first recorded sermon, in Matthew 5, with "Blessed are . . . [I hear a dramatic pause before he utters his next words] . . . the poor in spirit, for theirs is the kingdom of heaven" (v. 3).

Did you catch it? Do you think his listeners that day, gathered on the quiet, desolate hillside of Eremos, caught it? Jesus connected all that the law left us with—the curse—to the life that now exists for those who come to exist in him:

BLESSING.

He brought into view the opportunity to walk away from a cursed life and experience the wonder of a blessed one. This transition from curse to blessing is not just a theological concept; it represents a profound shift in the human condition. Where there was once condemnation and despair, Jesus introduced hope and renewal. He offers a new covenant, one that is based not on human ability to follow laws but on God's grace and the transformative power of faith in Christ.

Here's the fascinating thing about the word he chose with divine intentionality to declare first. "Blessed" in the original language would have been understood by those assembled that day as "happy." This choice of word is significant.

Over and over again, eight times, Jesus used the word "happy" in communicating how profoundly heaven's principles could affect our lives. Happiness, as Jesus described it, is not a fleeting emotion based on external circumstances but a deep, abiding sense of well-being that comes from a right relationship with God. The essence of his first message was how to be happy!

With this inaugural message, Jesus dropped a joy bomb.

This message, at the intersection of happiness and heaven, would disrupt the collective and individual spiritual paradigms in a way that would send shock waves through their souls, tremors through their teachings, and rivets through their religiosity. It detonated the possibility of a joy the money, entertainment, sex, pleasure, or success never could. This book will show you how to detonate that joy bomb in your own life, giving you the "codes" to unleash a joy beyond imagination.

WHO HIJACKED HAPPINESS?

When you flip through the pages of the Bible, you'll quickly notice that terms such as "happy," "joyful," and "blessed" seem to dance around one another, often used interchangeably to paint a picture of a life full of divine favor and contentment. It's as if they're three best friends on a mission to highlight the good life according to Scripture.

Take James, for instance, who didn't shy away from proclaiming that those who endure trials are "happy, spiritually prosperous, and favored by God" (1:12 AMP). This phrase might sound a bit grandiose, but it's spot-on. James 1:12 says, "Blessed is the one who perseveres under trial because, having stood the test, that person will receive the crown of life." Here, "blessed" isn't just a simple pat on the back; it's an acknowledgment of deep, enduring joy.

John Piper has said, "If you have nice little categories for 'joy is what Christians have' and 'happiness is what the world has,' you can scrap those when you go to the Bible, because the Bible is indiscriminate in its uses of the language of happiness and joy and contentment and satisfaction."[1] Joni Eareckson Tada echoes this sentiment, pointing out that Scripture uses these terms interchangeably along with words such as "delight," "gladness," and "blessed." She emphasizes that there is no scale of relative spiritual values applied to any of these.[2]

Then there's Psalm 1:1, which starts with "Blessed is the one who does not walk in step with the wicked." Swap out "blessed" for "happy" or "joyful" and the meaning remains rich and clear. The psalmist was celebrating a life aligned with divine wisdom, where happiness naturally follows.

Interestingly, the distinction between "happy" and "blessed" is a relatively new development in Christian thought. Traditionally, biblical texts did not differentiate between these states. The Hebrew word *asher* and the Greek word *makarios* are often translated as both "happy" and "blessed" in various contexts. So who hijacked the happiness we find in the Scriptures? This modern distinction might stem from an attempt to highlight the depth and divine origin of "blessedness" as opposed to the more everyday, fleeting notion of "happiness." This distinction, however, doesn't hold up when we examine Scripture closely.

Randy Alcorn, in an interview on the *Ask Pastor John* podcast, introduces a concept developed by pastor and author David Murray. Murray identified six kinds of happiness: nature happiness, social happiness, vocational happiness, physical happiness, intellectual happiness, and humor happiness. Alcorn says, "All of those, in God's common grace, are available to everyone, except the final one, which [Murray] calls 'spiritual happiness.'" This, according to Murray, is "a joy that at times contains more pleasure and delight than the other six put together."[3] Psalm 32:1 reflects this, using the Hebrew word *asher*: "Happy are those whose transgression is forgiven" (NRSVue) and in verse 2, "Happy are those to whom the Lord imputes no iniquity" (NRSVue). This happiness, rooted in reconciliation with God, transcends all others.[4]

In the Beatitudes, Jesus repeatedly declared people "blessed" in various states of life, from the poor in spirit to the peacemakers. Matthew 5:3–12 is a litany of blessings, each one promising joy despite circumstances that might not outwardly seem happy. Yet the underlying message is one of profound joy, a happiness rooted in spiritual fulfillment.[5]

Alcorn states: "When you find [happiness] in God, then you can look at nature and have greater pleasure in it. It is what [C. S.] Lewis talked about with the first things and the second things. . . . If you put the first things first, and the first thing is really the first person, who is God, then everything else falls in place."[6] Whether it's the unwavering joy of enduring faith, the simple happiness of righteous living, or the blessed assurance of divine favor, the Bible wraps these terms around a core truth: A life lived in harmony with God's will is a life overflowing with true happiness, joy, and blessing.[7]

This truth even flows into this very moment. Right now. Wherever you find yourself with these pages. It's not just I who wants you to know that you can be happy—God does too. Forget the scowl of the religious in their disdain for the idea of a "happy Christian." Set aside for a moment the idea that deep joy is based on your personality or emotional state. True joy, as Jesus presented it, is accessible to all, regardless of temperament or circumstance. Turn down the noise that fights to drown out the whisper that echoes throughout the vastness of your soul and tells you there is more. Not just more for someone else. More for you. More joy, fulfillment, purpose, freedom, possibility, and love than you could ever imagine.

You were wired to experience happiness because you were created by the God of infinite joy.

This divine wiring is not an accident; it reflects the very nature of God, who is the source of all true joy. Embracing this joy means aligning yourself with the reality of God's love and purpose for your life. It means stepping into a life that is defined not by the limitations of the old covenant but by the limitless possibilities of the new covenant in Christ.

How important to the heart of God must your joy be if it's the first thing Jesus spoke of in his first recorded sermon on planet Earth?

JOY BOMB

Your happiness *matters* to God.

Here's the truth: Where that joy comes from has been atrociously misattributed. What you will discover in the pages of this book is that Jesus is the singular source of happiness and that he has principles, ways of living, that not only bring happy feelings to us but create wells of deep joy within us.

Read the next portion of this book carefully; every page turned and word read is like a secret code that when punched in will trigger a detonation sequence sure to bring all your misconceptions about a joy-filled, happiness-fueled life crumbling to the ground. Here comes the joy bomb!

HAPPY ARE THE SPIRITUALLY BANKRUPT

Blessed are the poor in spirit, for theirs is the kingdom of heaven.

MATTHEW 5:3

THE TOPOGRAPHY OF JOY

I'm the proud dad of four incredible boys. Yes, four. Pray for Lorna and me! There's Kanaan Crue, Lawson Mayer, Navy Elliot, and Banner Paul. Within the first couple of years after having my oldest son, Kanaan, a friend shared an idea with me: Every five years he and his wife did something special and exclusive, a trip, with one of their children, since, like us, they had so many. I thought this was a great idea and couldn't wait for Kanaan's fifth birthday so we could take him on his five-year trip! The plan was that he would get to choose anywhere in the US he wanted to go, alone with Mom and Dad and, more importantly, away from his brothers. He loved the idea!

Little did I know he would choose the location of all locations, the trip of all trips—Disney World in Orlando, Florida. This set a precedent I didn't anticipate and was definitely not prepared for because, after Kanaan, Lawson wanted to go to Disney World, and then Navy, and, if history repeats itself, Banner will too! *What in the world have I gotten myself into?* So we've been to Disney multiple times now and we've had an amazing time. But it's always so interesting to observe that even there, at what has been dubbed "the happiest place on Earth," you see small children weeping, exhausted, and stomping their feet in disapproval of Mom and Dad's plans. This, of course, while Mom and Dad argue about which ride they should go on next and who was responsible for the sunscreen that was left behind. You can feel the irony in the reality that Disney is the home not only of Mickey Mouse and Tinker Bell but of melt-downs, bitter tears, and family feuds. The happiest place on Earth doesn't always live up to our expectations.

The truth is, there are expectations that we associate with certain locations. I believe that Jesus understood this prin-ciple when he chose the place from which he would deliver a powerful yet paradoxical message.

Jesus was very intentional about the spaces he occupied and the places he chose to be. In Matthew 5 we find Jesus beginning his ministry on a hillside, getting ready to teach his disciples, and the place he chose was the side of a mountain called Eremos, from a word meaning isolated, desolate, or strong.

Now, I have been a part of a few staff retreats and camps, and part of the magic is in the location. A great spot with a vibe in the city or a beautiful retreat in the mountains creates an elevated experience, but Jesus didn't choose a grand location. Quite the opposite. This setting was deliberately dedicated to the message he would teach, the message we have come to call the Beatitudes.

There's a good chance that you are somewhat familiar with this message:

> Blessed are the poor in spirit, for theirs is the kingdom
> of heaven.
> Blessed are those who mourn, for they will be comforted.

Blessed are the meek, for they will inherit the earth.

Blessed are those who hunger and thirst for
  righteousness, for they will be satisfied.

Blessed are the merciful, for they will be shown mercy.

Blessed are the pure in heart, for they will see God.

Blessed are the peacemakers, for they will be called
  children of God.

Blessed are those who are persecuted because
  of righteousness, for theirs is the kingdom of
  heaven.

Blessed are you when people insult you, persecute
  you and falsely say all kinds of evil against you
  because of me. (Matthew 5:3–11)

In the Beatitudes, Jesus shared eight life-changing ways of life. The translation we have says "blessed," but the word in its original form means happy or joyful.

This is wild. It's revolutionary. In Jesus's first recorded moment of public preaching, he told his followers how to be . . . happy? Not holy or reputable (although he would get to that later)—but happy. Oh, the self-made religious talking heads of our day wouldn't be able to get to their pulpits or YouTube soapboxes fast enough to upload a video and discredit the message and ministry of this new feel-good preacher! Jesus didn't start his message calling people out or talking about sin; he was giving them keys to joy. Heresy! The question it really suggests for me is this: How important must people's experiencing the joy of the Lord be if God himself chose this topic to address first? Not only that, but we cannot forget that the place he chose to hand us the keys to joy, Eremos, was a place of both desolation and strength.

Jesus uses the topography to illustrate the topic and reveal the tension in this truth: *the strength God gives through joy can be produced in desolate places.* That reveals to us that our joy is not dependent on a structure, a system, or circumstances. It also declares that joy can be found in isolated places. It's not determined by people, possessions, or popularity. He's pointing us to a notion that's hard for us to grasp—that happiness has little to do with what we have or where we are.

Let's look more closely at where Jesus taught from. Hills and mountains were significant in the history of the people he was speaking to. Throughout the Bible, mountains often symbolize places of divine revelation and encounter. For instance, Mount Sinai holds profound importance as it was the site where God gave the law to Moses. The dramatic events on Sinai, where the law was etched on tablets for Moses to carry to the people, are detailed in Exodus 19–20. This moment marked the establishment of the covenant between God and Israel, emphasizing the sacred and binding nature of God's commandments.

Another crucial mountain is Mount Zion, which became a symbol of the very church that Christ would build. Zion is frequently mentioned in the Psalms and the Prophets as a place of divine dwelling and ultimate redemption. Psalm 2:6 declares, "I have installed my king on Zion, my holy mountain." In the

New Testament the writer of Hebrews also referred to Mount Zion, describing it as the "city of the living God, the heavenly Jerusalem" (12:22), symbolizing the ultimate gathering of God's people and the establishment of his kingdom.

Jesus's ministry was connected to mountains and hills as well. He often sought the solitude of hills for prayer and teaching. One of the most poignant connections is Golgotha, the hill where Jesus was crucified, fulfilling his mission to redeem humanity (Luke 23:33). Before this ultimate sacrifice, Jesus proclaimed his message from various elevated places, symbolizing the higher spiritual perspectives he offered.

Mountains in the Bible are not just geographical features; they represent moments when heaven and earth met, where God revealed his purposes, and where significant spiritual truths were imparted. In choosing these locations, God underscored their importance in the narrative of faith. This pattern continued with Jesus, whose teachings from hillsides and mountains echoed the profound significance of these elevated places in biblical history. His Sermon on the Mount, for example, is one of his most famous discourses, providing a new law that emphasizes inner righteousness over mere external behavior (Matthew 5–7).

So the association of God with mountains and hilltops highlights the idea of elevation—not just physical elevation, but spiritual elevation, calling people to a higher understanding for a deeper relationship with the divine. This moment in Jesus's ministry, his teaching the Beatitudes from an elevated place, is in perfect continuity with the rich biblical symbolism as he invited his followers to see life, faith, and spirituality from a vantage point aligned with God's perspective.

It's important to note that Jesus's teachings came from a higher perspective, one that we often lack. Jesus could "see" something that the world couldn't. I am talking about his divine perspective—one that goes far beyond human understanding. He wasn't limited by time, place, or circumstance. He saw not only what was happening in front of him but also the eternal implications and hidden layers behind every situation. His view stretched across the past, present, and future, connecting moments in a way we often miss. This is reinforced by the image of the story: Jesus sat above the people as the hillside sloped downward, placing them beneath him. From his vantage point, Jesus could see far beyond the people, but the people looking up at him could see only Jesus. In other words, they didn't share Jesus's broader perspective; they simply saw him. They couldn't see all that he could see, but they could see him. This is a beautiful picture for our lives because, most of the time, we can't see what Jesus sees. We don't have the vantage point he has. As high as the heavens are above the earth, so are his ways above ours (Isaiah 55:9). But what we can see, when we can't see, is Jesus. We look to Jesus, who is the author and perfecter of our faith (Hebrews 12:2). Through his teaching we get to see the world and our lives through his eyes.

This picture speaks to us today because, let's face it, most of the time we don't have Jesus's perspective. We're usually wrapped up in whatever's right in front of us, trying to make sense of our own little slice of the moment. But Jesus? He sees our lives with a much bigger, broader understanding. While we're staring at a single piece of the puzzle, he's looking at the whole thing put together.

Think about it. Maybe you're in a job you're not thrilled about, but you need it to pay the bills. It's easy to feel stuck and frustrated and wonder why you're there. Jesus, though, can see how this job could be laying the groundwork for a future opportunity you can't even imagine yet. He knows the people you're meeting, what skills you're learning, and how all of that might fit into his bigger plan for you down the road.

Or think about your relationships. Have you ever had a relationship that ended, leaving you feeling hurt and con- fused? In the moment it's hard to understand why something like that would happen, and all you can see is the pain right in front of you. But Jesus can see the long-term picture. Maybe he knows this separation will help you grow, or maybe he's preparing someone new to come into your life who will bring a whole new level of empathy and support you never knew you needed.

Then there are those times when we face health challenges—something that's slowing us down or making life feel a lot harder. We naturally focus on the discomfort and start worrying about what this might mean for our future. But Jesus has the bigger view here too. He sees how this season could bring us closer to people who understand what we're going through or how it might strengthen our faith in ways we never imagined.

These everyday moments remind us that even when we don't see the full picture, we can still look to Jesus. When we can't see what's ahead, we can still see him, and that's what really matters.

Now, I want to point out something I find encouraging. Jesus and the crowds that came to him didn't ascend to the pinnacle of this mountain, which could represent the highest heights of success, affluence, or influence. But they weren't at the very bottom of the mountain in a low place either, which could represent a place of defeat, failure, or insignificance. The place Jesus chose to give a master class on joy was somewhere in the middle, somewhere fairly underwhelming and, well, ordinary. Some would even say it was less of a mountain and more of a hill. No, there was nothing about the situation that was spectacular, but just because it wasn't spectacular doesn't mean it was insignificant.

Consider the simplicity of a conversation over a cup of coffee with a friend. You might be discussing everyday things, yet one sentence or piece of advice could have a profound effect on you. Or think about how you show faithfulness at work, completing daily tasks with a good attitude. These actions might seem mundane, but they often lead to personal growth, recognition, and unexpected opportunities. There have been times I've been doing something as simple as taking a walk and suddenly experienced a moment when God gave me divine direction for my life. These moments illustrate how the miraculous can happen in the mundane.

We often rob ourselves of life's most significant moments

because we have been convinced that something extraordinary or spectacular must take place for something to be supernatural and significant. Jesus illustrated that it *can* happen like that, but also that the miracles of life happen in the mundanity of life. In the Beatitudes, Jesus was communicating one of the most important truths we will discover in this life: Joy is generated from within. Our external surroundings do not have the power to bring us joy. Happiness is ignited within our spirits. When Jesus points to joy, he first points us inward, to our spirits (John 15:11; Galatians 5:22).

Just as Jesus gave powerful words to his followers in a desolate place, we can find strength in our empty places too. These experiences can strip away superficial sources of happiness and help us discover a deeper, more resilient joy that is not dependent on what's happening around us but on what God is doing within us. By turning inward and connecting with the Spirit of God, we can ignite a joy that is rooted in our inner strength and faith, providing us with the resilience to navigate life's toughest challenges.

THE PARADOX OF JOY

This is a truth we see repeatedly in Scripture but one that is always being challenged by our humanity.

We think we can get joy. In fact, we have been programmed to believe that happiness is something that can be siphoned from an earthly source. Multimillion-dollar marketing campaigns coined as "joy marketing" pervade the culture. Companies have discovered that 93 percent of Americans are on a quest to find joy in their lives.[1] With advertising slogans such as Coca-Cola's "Open a Coke, open happiness" or McDonald's "I'm lovin' it," the message is clear.

These campaigns tap into a fundamental human desire for happiness and satisfaction, presenting their products as shortcuts to these emotions. The idea is that by consuming their products, we can instantly experience joy. This notion is both compelling and misleading. It suggests that joy is something external that can be bought and consumed, rather than an internal state that we cultivate through our thoughts, actions, and relationships.

The prevalence of these types of marketing strategies raises questions about the impact on our collective psyche. If joy is continually portrayed as something that can be purchased, it may lead to a consumerist mindset by which we constantly seek external validation and gratification. This can result in a cycle of temporary happiness followed by inevitable disappointment when the initial thrill fades, prompting us to buy more in search of the next fix.

Long before joy was positioned as a commodity by commercials, ads, and efforts that drove us to empty places promising lasting joy that never came, there has been the broken compass of the human heart, guiding us to much of the same.

Remember the story of Abraham and Sarah? Sarah, unable to have children, found herself in a state of deep despair that led her to a scandalous decision. In their desperation the couple tried to solve their problem by seeking joy externally through Sarah's servant Hagar (Genesis 16:1–4). Hagar conceived and bore a child, but this situation didn't bring the joy they had hoped for; instead, it created turmoil and heartache, weaving an endless web of difficulty and strife within their household that has created generations of conflict (Genesis 16:5–6).

Eventually, God miraculously intervened. Sarah finally became pregnant, fulfilling God's promise (Genesis 21:1–2). This miraculous event was a testament to the joy bomb that God ignites when we trust in divine timing. Similarly, when we yearn for joy, we often look outside ourselves and God's provision, seeking it in transient, external things. But true joy doesn't come from the outside in. As Isaac, Sarah's long-awaited son, grew within her, so joy flourishes from the inside out, nurtured by faith and prepared through patience (Genesis 21:6–7).

Let's sharpen our focus a bit on the opening words of Jesus's message: "Blessed are the poor in spirit, for theirs is the kingdom of heaven" (Matthew 5:3).

Happy are the "poor" in spirit. At first glance this may seem paradoxical. How can being poor in spirit lead to joy? To understand this we need to delve deeper into what it means to be poor in spirit.

Being poor in spirit means recognizing our own spiritual poverty and our utter dependence on God. It is an acknowledgment that we are insufficient and that we need God's grace and mercy in every aspect of our lives. This recognition of our neediness allows us to let go of pride and self-reliance and open our hearts to receive the fullness of God's blessings.

Oswald Chambers once wrote, "The knowledge of our own poverty brings us to the moral frontier where Jesus Christ works."[2] This profound insight highlights the transformative power of recognizing our limitations and spiritual insufficiency. By acknowledging our own poverty, we come to the end of ourselves and stand at the threshold of divine intervention. This "moral frontier" is the point where human effort and pride cease and we become fully open to the work of Jesus Christ. It is here that Jesus meets us, not with condemnation for our inadequacies, but with grace and redemption. At this frontier we experience the beginning of true spiritual growth and renewal as we allow Christ to work within us, shaping us into the people God intended us to be. This is a place of deep humility, where we understand that our strength is found not in our own abilities but in our dependence on him. Chambers's words remind us that spiritual poverty is not a state of despair but a gateway to the transformative and redemptive work of the Holy Spirit in our lives (Matthew 5:3; 2 Corinthians 12:9–10). By embracing our spiritual poverty, we invite Jesus to fill our emptiness with his presence and power. It is a continuous journey of surrender, where we move beyond mere moral striving into a relationship characterized by faith, trust, and reliance on God's grace. In this place of humble dependence, we find the true essence of Christian living and the fullness of life that Jesus promised (John 10:10).

When we are poor in spirit, we are able to receive joy because we are not trying to manufacture it ourselves through external circumstances or achievements. Instead, we understand that true joy comes from a personal relationship with God. This joy is not contingent on our situations or possessions but is rooted in the assurance of God's love for us.

The spirit that acknowledges consistent dependency on God is the spirit that is filled with joy. This is because such a spirit is constantly connected to the source of all joy—God himself. When we live in this state of dependency, we experience the peace and contentment that comes from trusting in God's plan and provision.

It's important to understand that what we lack is just as significant as what we possess. This shift in perspective is essential if we are to acknowledge that there are some things only God can generate in our lives. Even if we were to possess much of what the world offers and become rich by cultural standards, we could still find ourselves spiritually bankrupt. The truth is, we are all poor in some area. We don't have the ability to save ourselves, so we rejoice in a Savior who came to save us. We don't have the ability to forgive, redeem, and sanctify ourselves by any means, so we rejoice in the reality that Jesus forgives, redeems, and sanctifies us.

A poignant example of spiritual bankruptcy is found in the story of the rich young ruler (Mark 10:17–27). This man approached Jesus seeking the way to eternal life. He was wealthy, respected, and morally upright, adhering to all the commandments from his youth. But when Jesus told him to sell all his possessions, give the money to the poor, and follow him, the young ruler went away sad. He lacked the willingness to surrender fully to God. His wealth was a barrier, and this interaction revealed his spiritual poverty despite his material abundance.

Being rich in knowledge, wealth, or relationships can't bring us the same joy as the eternal promise of heaven does. This joy comes from being poor in spirit, as we recognize our need for God and experience the fullness of his love and grace. It is this humble, dependent spirit that unlocks the door to lasting and profound joy. The story of the rich young ruler teaches us that no matter how much we possess in worldly terms, or how much religious equity we have invested in even minute spiritual disciplines or principles, we fall short of what is required to inherit the kingdom of God. True richness comes from acknowledging our spiritual need and embracing the transformative power of God's grace.

It can't be overlooked that Scripture uses the term "inherit" to describe the transfer of spiritual wealth from God to his children (Mark 10:17). "Inherit" implies an act of transfer based on relationship, not to be confused with wages that comes from works. Jesus is leading our souls to the reality that God allows us to receive his kingdom based on our relationship with him and nothing else.

In an interview the great NBA center Shaquille O'Neal jokingly said of his multimillion-dollar fortune, "I told my kids, 'We ain't rich, I'm rich!'"[3] implying that just because they are his kids doesn't mean they have what he has. The good news for the knowingly bankrupt children of God is that he is gracious and generous, and everything he possesses he pours into our hearts and lives! As it says in Ephesians 1:3, "Praise be to the God and Father of our Lord Jesus Christ, who has blessed us in the heavenly realms with every spiritual blessing in Christ."

THE PROSPECTS FOR JOY

It feels as though it was just a few short years ago when I turned in my sixth-grade paper, struggling to answer a question that was too complicated for a twelve-year-old to fully understand and express. Our assignment was to answer "What do you want to be when you grow up?" Admittedly, I've already asked my boys, all younger now than I was then, the same question. Somehow our answers fell into the same category: professional athlete. Inspired by stars such as Grant Hill, my favorite at the time (I am from Michigan—go Pistons!), and Michael Jordan, what twelve-year-old boy didn't want to be an NBA star? I proudly turned in my paper, confidently professing my aspirations as a future pro with a grin on my face. I was shocked when that paper was returned to me with a big red *F* at the top, circled twice for added emphasis, I guess. When I asked my teacher why my effort received a failing grade, he said it was "unrealistic" and that I did not take the assignment seriously. His wasn't the best approach for inspiring the next generation to dream, but I don't hold anything against him. The truth is, there were some natural qualities I lacked to achieve such a lofty ambition, height being at the top of the list!

Our natural response to these types of deficits is to create an against-all-odds, if-you-can-dream-it-you-can-achieve-it attitude. I am all about that! Yet, at the same time, our deficits give us just as many clues about our destiny as our strengths do. Some achieve despite what they lack; others rise in light of it. Acknowledging what we don't have gives us the awareness to sharpen our focus on what we do. And, at times, what we lack creates space for God to fill our lives with his supernatural power and possibilities.

This is certainly true in our spiritual lives. Throughout Scripture we see God using what people like you and me lacked as a catalyst to display his wonder in their stories. The examples are almost too many to count! A shepherd boy didn't measure up to his brothers, the king, or the giant, but God made up the difference for David (1 Samuel 16–17). The adopted son of a pharaoh had an identity crisis, blind spots in leadership, and speech problems, yet Moses was handpicked by God to lead (Exodus 2–4). A woman with just a little oil and flour realized that her greatest asset was her emptiness, and that oil flowed until it filled every pot she could find (1 Kings 17:8–16). Another woman came to Jesus with the deficit of a terrible reputation, but she worshipped at Jesus's feet, and he declared that wherever the gospel was preached in the world, she would be remembered not for her past but for her praise (Luke 7:36–50). In another instance, while other women donned their heels, rare jewels, and makeup, Esther wowed the royal court and won the king's affection with her natural beauty (Esther 1–10). The Scripture is loaded with stories of people who, when evaluated against their odds or compared to others, were found wanting, and still God beautifully filled their empty spaces with his glory.

As I reflect on these biblical narratives, I can't help but draw parallels to my own life and the lives of those around me. We often focus so much on what we lack that we forget to see the bigger picture. We forget that our deficiencies can be the very things that lead us to our true calling. Think about it: How many times have you felt inadequate, only to realize later that those very inadequacies led you to a path you might not have otherwise considered? It's as if our weaknesses are guiding lights, redirecting us to where we're meant to be.

When I think about my own journey, it's clear that my perceived shortcomings have shaped who I am today. I didn't grow up to be an NBA star, but I found other passions and talents that I might not have explored if I had been solely focused on one unrealistic dream. It's in the exploration of these other paths that we find our strengths, capabilities, and callings.

In the end it's about perspective. We can view our deficits as obstacles or opportunities. The difference lies in how we choose to respond to them. Will we let them discourage us, or will we let them lead us to new and unexpected places? Will we focus on what we lack, or will we embrace the journey of discovering what we possess?

Embracing this perspective brings joy in the realization

that our lives are unfolding according to a greater plan, in which even our weaknesses and setbacks play a crucial role. This joy comes not from achieving perfection or meeting society's expectations but from understanding and accepting that God's purpose for us transcends our limitations. It's in this understanding that we find true happiness—a happiness that comes from aligning ourselves with God's will and discovering the unique path he has laid out for each of us.

So the next time you feel disheartened by your shortcomings, remember the stories of David, Moses, the widow of Zarephath, Esther, and the woman who anointed Jesus. Remember that God uses our weaknesses to show his strength. And remember that sometimes what we think we want isn't what we need. Our true calling might be just around the corner, hidden in the very areas where we feel we lack the most. Trust the process, embrace your journey, and let your deficits guide you to your destiny.

It comes as no surprise, then, that as Jesus began his earthly ministry, meeting all kinds of people, he chose twelve young men with various shortcomings and deficiencies. He could have picked kings and influencers, the wealthy and the charming, but he chose the least likely to change the world. The disciples we've come to know and admire were not impressive people. We know that all of these young men had gone "spiritually undrafted," or unqualified to serve and lead by every religious standard of their day.

Jewish boys would begin memorizing the Torah, the first five books of what we call the Old Testament, early in their lives and throughout their adolescence. They would then either be chosen to continue studying with a rabbi or be rejected from further study and commissioned to learn their father's trade. So the fact that Peter, James, John, Matthew, Andrew, and the other disciples were working in their fathers' trades gives us the insight that these men had been rejected, in a sense, from the prospect of becoming "holy men."

The good news for them and the good news for us is that this is exactly who God gives his kingdom to: not the polished, accomplished, or spiritually elite, but people who can readily admit who they are not, what they lack, and where they come up short.

It's a powerful reminder that God doesn't call the qualified; he qualifies the called. In choosing those who seemed least capable, Jesus demonstrated that it's not about our abilities but about our availability to his will. Each disciple brought something unique to the table despite his imperfections. Peter's passion, though sometimes misguided, became a cornerstone of the early church. Matthew, a tax collector despised by his own people, showed that redemption and transformation are possible for anyone. James and John, known as the "Sons of Thunder" for their fiery tempers, became voices of love and commitment.

Their stories remind us that our past does not define our future in God's kingdom. It doesn't matter where we've been or how many times we've failed; what matters is our willingness to follow and trust in his plan. The disciples' journey with Jesus was filled with growth, mistakes, and learning moments, much like our spiritual journeys. They walked beside him, witnessed miracles, and slowly transformed into the pillars of faith.

The disciples, with their humble beginnings and lack of spiritual accolades, epitomized the beatitude of Matthew 5:3. They were poor in spirit, acknowledging their need for God and their dependence on him. It is precisely this recognition of our own insufficiency and God's sufficiency that opens the door to the kingdom of heaven.

So as we reflect on these ordinary men chosen for an extraordinary mission, let's find encouragement in knowing that God sees potential in each of us, even when we don't see it in ourselves. He calls us to step out in faith, embrace our shortcomings, and allow his strength to be made perfect in our weakness. Just as the disciples did, we, too, can become instruments of his love and grace, influencing the world in ways we never imagined. In our humility and poverty of spirit we find the true richness of his kingdom.

The Sermon on the Mount offers insights more valuable than the rarest treasures. When I read Scripture, I always note the spaces and places Jesus chose to occupy, knowing that everything he did and everywhere he went was intentional. I also consider the audience and the implications of what he was saying for the people in his presence when he spoke. What were they feeling, hearing, and seeing in light of their personal lives, history, culture, paradigms, and expectations? When these factors are considered, many of Jesus's words hit differently. Then, of course, I ask, *What are the implications for me?*

There were likely at least two audiences present that day on Eremos to hear Jesus speak. One was the disciples. These followers of Jesus were not on the same religious, political, or societal levels as the other group present: the Pharisees and religious leaders. So two groups of people were hearing one message in at least two different ways as Jesus declared, "Blessed are the poor in spirit, for theirs is the kingdom of heaven."

For the disciples these words might have been incredibly empowering and comforting. They were often marginalized and overlooked by the society around them, struggling with their own doubts and spiritual poverty. Hearing that the kingdom of heaven belonged to them would have been a profound affirmation of their worth. This message would have strengthened their resolve and deepened their commitment to following Jesus.

On the other hand, the Pharisees and religious leaders likely interpreted Jesus's words through a different lens. Accustomed to viewing themselves as the spiritual elite, they might have felt challenged or even threatened by Jesus's assertion that the kingdom of heaven was accessible to those who were poor in spirit. This was a radical departure from the prevailing religious thought that emphasized strict adherence to the law and ritual purity as pathways to God's favor.

The Sermon on the Mount is a call to a radical transformation of the heart and mind. It invites us to embrace a new way of living that transcends societal norms and expectations, challenging us to live with greater compassion, humility, and love.

For the religious leaders to hear these words associated with the kingdom of heaven was certainly infuriating. This is when they realized that Jesus was a problem. With these words and this belief, he was undermining everything for which they had worked. The idea of being poor in spirit indicated that the kingdom of heaven was not accessed by the mere study of the Torah, memorization of teachings, or ostentatious offerings or prayers. It disrupted their belief that their coveted status in society would eventually be traded in for status in heaven.

They were offended by the idea that to inherit this kingdom you had to get low, decrease, and take joyful inventory of what you lacked. Neither achievement nor affluence nor adulation was the price of admission into this party. No, for the first time they realized that they weren't as great of candidates for the kingdom as they had thought.

This message hit the rest of those gathered on the hillside—namely, the disciples—differently. For them this was the best thing they had ever heard! After being rejected in so many ways, there was now a path to acceptance and purpose. They were "undrafted" but got to walk on with a scholarship they didn't qualify for and take their place in the kingdom.

When the prevailing religious belief perpetuated the idea that it was who you were and what you had done that justified you for a position in the kingdom, Jesus reoriented his listeners to the truth that no matter who you are or what you've done, the joy of belonging to the kingdom is yours!

This is the lesson for us today: The kingdom of God is available to us, here and now, regardless of our status or position or place in society. When you take in *that* truth and make it real to your heart, you've activated the first code to unleash the joy bomb in your own life.

CODE TWO

HAPPY ARE THE DESPERATELY SAD

Blessed are those who mourn,

for they will be comforted.

MATTHEW 5:4

JOY IN THE MOURNING

I remember a few weeks after getting married when I hopped out of a tour bus in the middle of nowhere, USA, and my phone rang. My beautiful bride of no more than six weeks was on the other end. Her voice was broken, reflecting her heartache as she told me that her dad, my new father-in-law, had been diagnosed with leukemia.

The complexity of the issues would only compound over the coming months with the crushing weight of more bad news. In what seemed like an instant, the first year of our marriage, which we thought would be nothing but the breath-taking views of a mountaintop experience, was thrown into a valley. We had no control over it.

There is a tension in which we all exist, and it's the pull between two realities that create the topography of human life: joy and grief. We might experience these as brokenness and wholeness, frustration and elation, success and failure. High mountains and deep valleys are all part of the terrain of our journey. We can't go around them. Only through.

I know that you've felt this tension at some point in your life. At times, even in the same moment, we can be caught with something joyous in our hearts while something grieves us within our souls. I'm sure you've fought some battles and won and, at other times, fought and lost. I'm sure you've experienced great successes and joys in your life and felt the crushing blow of disappointment and distress. We can laugh to the point of tears and shout in celebration while simultaneously we are at the end of our rope on the inside. There is an undeniable coexistence of both pain and hope.

The unfortunate truth is that there is no life that sorrow leaves untouched. Although God is supremely good, faithful, and kind, the Scripture holds no promise for a pain-free life. Every individual, at some point, encounters moments of pain and sadness. Life is a tapestry woven with both wonder and wounds, joy and sorrow. What defines our journey is the choice we make in focusing on these elements—whether we choose to gaze at the wonder or stare into the wounds.

If we choose well, we can trigger a joy bomb—a burst of pure, concentrated wonder that suddenly fills the atmosphere. Joy bombs can show up in moments of beauty and peace, or even as subtle reminders of God's love. But just as a burst of joy explodes, our focus determines whether that joy fades or stays. If we focus on the wounds instead, we may be tempted to think of joy as fleeting or insignificant, dismissing it as merely a temporary diversion. But the principle at work here is that joy can have lasting effects on our perspective—if we choose to let it. By embracing these moments of joy and wonder, even amid challenges, we gain the strength and hope to move forward.

The story of Thomas in John 20:24–29 illustrates this tension:

Now Thomas (also known as Didymus), one of the Twelve, was not with the disciples when Jesus came. So the other disciples told him, "We have seen the Lord!" But he said to them, "Unless I see the nail marks in his hands and put my finger where the nails were, and put my hand into his side, I will not believe."

A week later his disciples were in the house again, and Thomas was with them. Though the doors were locked, Jesus came and stood among them and said, "Peace be with you!" Then he said to Thomas, "Put your finger here; see my hands. Reach out your hand and put it into my side. Stop doubting and believe."

Thomas said to him, "My Lord and my God!"

Then Jesus told him, "Because you have seen me, you have believed; blessed are those who have not seen and yet have believed."

Isn't it interesting that after the disciple Thomas witnessed the astonishing wonder of Jesus walking through a wall, he still desired to see, touch, and feel the wounds of Jesus? Despite witnessing a miraculous event, Thomas was still compelled to verify the physical wounds of Christ. He glanced at the wonder but stared at the wounds. This action earned him the moniker "Doubting Thomas." Thomas's story is a powerful reminder of human nature: He was fixated on what was wrong instead of being fascinated by what was wonderful. Thomas wanted what he felt to be proof for his faith. But joy is not a feeling—it's a focus.

This tendency is common in many of us. We often allow our attention to be captured by our struggles, pain, and doubts instead of embracing the beauty and miracles that also exist in our lives. Thomas had the opportunity to be captivated by the extraordinary—Jesus's ability to transcend physical barriers; the fact that the crucified Christ stood before him, resurrected, and cared enough about him to make his presence uniquely known to him. But instead of relying on what he could hear, the familiar voice of the Master, and even though he could look into the very eyes of the Christ, he needed to *feel* it for it to be true. This reflects a broader human condition in which the negative often overshadows the positive in our perceptions. The miracle gets lost in the midst of our logic and emotions, and we allow what we feel to be the greatest indicator of truth we experience. Jesus was gracious with Thomas, allowing him to feel what he perceived as evidence of the truth. However, this isn't always the case. If we surrender to the idea of living solely from our feelings, we risk losing sight of the truth of who God is and who we are in him.

Reflecting on this, we can learn to shift our focus. Like a joy bomb that briefly explodes with light, moments of wonder are given to us to keep our spirits ignited. We can choose to glance at our wounds and stare into the wonder, creating a more permanent perspective of faith and hope. It's not about ignoring the pain or pretending it doesn't exist; rather, it's about recognizing the full spectrum of our experiences and deciding where to place our emphasis.

Thomas's story is not just about doubt but about the

human proclivity to seek out and dwell on the tangible evidence of hardship. It challenges us to elevate our gaze, to embrace wonder and let it illuminate our path, even when we experience the inevitable wounds of life. And, in doing so, we are reminded that while sorrow may touch every life, joy is a more powerful force, holding us up and propelling us forward.

Now, on the other hand, we must also examine one of the greatest misconceptions in the Christian faith, which I touched on earlier, and that is that all believers only feel or should only always *feel* happy. Many believers are held hostage by this mindset, which is not aligned with Scripture. This misconception is like a shadow looming over our understanding of God's character and the truth of Scripture.

Have you ever heard someone "quote the Bible" only to misquote it with a saying that's not really in the Bible? It's usually something like this: "Well, the Bible says, 'He'll never put more on us than we can bear.'" It's said so genuinely and with the intention to encourage, yet it is more likely to be found on a fortune cookie than in the Word of God. This kind of misinformation perpetuates wrong beliefs about some of the realities of following Jesus. If we don't read Scripture correctly, we can't see God correctly. If we don't see God correctly, we won't interpret the circumstances of our lives correctly. This is why "Blessed are those who mourn, for they will be comforted" (Matthew 5:4) can be difficult to understand.

The first reality this scripture directs our attention toward is that we will mourn. It's supported by other scriptures that say things such as "Weeping may endure for a night, but joy comes in the morning" (Psalm 30:5 NKJV); "In this world you will have trouble. But take heart! I have overcome the world" (John 16:33); and "The LORD is close to the brokenhearted and saves those who are crushed in spirit" (Psalm 34:18). Many of us carry guilt and shame because of the depths of sadness, disappointment, or pain we have felt—leaving us in a mourning that we can't seem to pull ourselves from, and we think that feeling is wrong. This is the furthest thing from what the Bible unveils to us about pain.

Think about it like this: Sorrow and joy are two sides of the same coin, both a part of the currency of our human experience. I can't point you to any people God used in his kingdom who did not have moments of great sorrow or experience the cold grip of loss and pain. They were not thrown away by God or disqualified by him for feeling it. David prayed, "Do not cast me from your presence or take your Holy Spirit from me" (Psalm 51:11). As much as David understood God's heart, he didn't realize that God doesn't just throw us out on our worst days or in our worst seasons of life. We often look at pain, grief, or even failure as a door God won't walk through. The truth is, he will, but we must open it.

Life is often like the ocean, with its vast expanse and unpredictable nature. On the surface the waves can be choppy and tumultuous, representing the challenges and uncertainties we face daily. These waves may symbolize the stress, anxiety, and trials that threaten to overwhelm us. But beneath this restless surface lies a deep undercurrent of joy and peace, which we can access through our faith in Christ. This undercurrent represents the unwavering flow of God's goodness and love, which sustains us even in the most difficult times.

Through Christ we find the strength to navigate life's storms. His teachings and sacrifice provide us with a foundation of hope and resilience. By anchoring ourselves in the depths of God's grace, we remain secure and grounded, preventing us from drifting into perilous waters. This anchor symbolizes our faith, which keeps us steadfast and immovable, no matter how fierce the storm.

As it says in Hebrews 6:19, "We have this hope as an anchor for the soul, firm and secure." This scripture beautifully captures the essence of our faith. It is this hope, anchored in the promise of God's grace and salvation, that keeps us safe and steady. We are reminded that no matter how chaotic the surface of our lives may appear, we can always find refuge and stability in our faith.

In moments of doubt or fear, it is crucial to remember the deeper truths of our spiritual journey. Just as an anchor holds a ship in place, our faith holds us firmly in the embrace of God's love. By trusting in his plan and relying on his grace, we can face any storm with confidence and peace, knowing that we are anchored in the unwavering goodness of God.

In his inaugural sermon, Jesus shared a powerful message that offers hope and comfort, especially to those who are grieving. He said, "Blessed are those who mourn, for they will be comforted." This idea, as discussed in *Kingdom Ethics* by David P. Gushee and Glen H. Stassen, points to a deeper reality: God is gracious and actively working to deliver us from our sorrows and transform our mourning into joy.[1]

Instead of seeing mourning as something negative, Jesus encourages us to view it as a process filled with divine promise. When we grieve, it's not just a sad experience; it's a moment when God is particularly close to us, offering comfort and healing. The belief that God collects our tears and is present in our pain reassures us that our sorrow isn't ignored or overlooked. God is using our mourning to deliver us from mourning, guiding us out of despair and into joy.

Instead of being a distant observer, God is intimately involved in our struggles. Psalm 34:18 reinforces this by saying, "The LORD is close to the brokenhearted and saves those who are crushed in spirit." This means that God doesn't just watch our suffering from afar; he is right there with us, catching our tears and acknowledging our pain. Our disappointments become divine transportation, lifting us out of the pit of despair and leading us into better days.

Get ready for a joy bomb! God has given us the act of mourning to transform our spirit from a state of despair into a sacred space where God works within our sorrow to bring about soul-soothing comfort. Mourning is not about quickly moving past our sadness or trying to please God by being happy again. Instead, it is about God meeting us in our pain, validating our grief, and gently guiding us toward healing and better days.

Understanding this changes how we experience grief. We

can embrace our mourning with the confidence that God isn't waiting for us to get over our sadness. He is actively involved in our journey through it, offering a sense of hope. Our tears are seen and valued by a compassionate God, who uses our grief to bring us closer to his comfort and joy. So, in our deepest sorrows, we can find solace in knowing that God is right there with us, transforming our mourning into an experience of divine comfort and better days ahead.

NO CRYING IN CHRISTIANITY?

In his book *The Voice of the Heart*, Chip Dodd shares an incredible insight that changed my life. He teaches that everyone has eight core emotions: hurt, lonely, sad, anger, fear, shame, guilt, and glad.[2] These eight core emotions are doorways into experiencing aspects of God's character. If we allow ourselves to fully experience these emotions, we may find that they lead us to a deeper understanding of God's compassion, love, and grace. Embracing our emotions, rather than suppressing them, opens us up to the richness of a genuine relationship with God.

Moreover, acknowledging these emotions allows us to connect more authentically with others. When we share our grief, others feel permission to share theirs. When we express our joy, it can be contagious, spreading hope and light. This authenticity is where true community and fellowship are built. It's where we find that we are not alone in our struggles and that joy, even when intertwined with grief, can be a powerful force for healing and unity.

My mom was recently in Austin over the holidays, and we were talking about shows and movies we watched and enjoyed when I was a kid. Her favorite was *A League of Their Own*. It's known for the famous line, "Are you crying? Is she crying? There's no crying . . . There's no crying in baseball!" Some of us have made this a deeper personal mantra—even those in church services on Sundays tightly grip the seat back in front of us during a powerful moment of prayer, a worship song, or a message, fighting to hold back the very tears and emotion God wired us with to deliver us from our hurts. We often don't permit ourselves to feel pain, disappointment, regret, or loss. We tell ourselves there's no room for what have been labeled as negative emotions in Christian spirituality. There's no "crying" in Christianity. Culture will tell us there are no emotions expressed in true manhood. The church often sends the message that our emotions are to be checked at the door. The world will give us plenty of options to numb pain rather than feel it. We avoid, ignore, or mismanage our pain. It takes vulnerability and a willingness to feel our hurts and to allow ourselves to be truly comforted. Vulnerability opens the door to the healing comfort of God.

I remember the first time my friend showed me a new reality show that aired briefly on MTV called *If You Really Knew Me*. The showrunners had groups of students from across the country fill in the blank and tell their stories. Their hope was to end bullying through understanding, thinking that if students knew one another's struggles, they'd be more likely to express compassion rather than criticism to one another. The show would gather all the students in the school gym, and instructors would have them stand in a line along one wall. Then one of the instructors would read from a list of statements—things such as "If you really knew me, you'd know . . . that I grew up in a broken home," or "that I've been a victim of abuse," or "that I sometimes feel lonely and scared, even among friends." For each statement that a student identified with, he or she would take a step forward, and eventually all the students would cross a line in the middle of the room.

Then the instructor would ask them to look around. With tears in their eyes, they would see their peers—people whom they had overlooked or prejudged—and realize that they were all stuck in similar struggles.

Now, this all took place in a school, so, assuming they had no relationship with Jesus, it was no real surprise that most of the students would have lives riddled with the unfortunate fractures of sin. But I'll never forget the day my friend used this very approach at the end of a message he was preaching to a thousand students at a church youth conference. Surely, I thought, the result would be different in a room full of church kids; however, as he made penetrating statements such as "If you really knew me, you'd know I struggle with an addiction," students stepped forward. "If you really knew me, you'd know I have been sexually abused." Students stepped forward. "If you really knew me, you'd know I've contemplated suicide." Students stepped forward. "If you really knew me, you'd know

I've felt deep rejection." Before long, more than half the seats were empty and the altar was full. I think everyone could have stepped forward, but some remained seated, clinging to the false sense of comfort that superficiality can create.

The truth is, we are all wrestling. We all have stories none of us want to tell but wish everyone knew. We aren't just defined by our brokenness; we are silenced by it. We convince ourselves that hiding is better than healing. If we are ever going to be comforted, we have to be real. We would rather bury our brokenness or loss and be a prisoner of it than reveal our brokenness and be comforted in it.

I've come to the unfortunate realization that many of us have bought into a version of Christianity that has trained us to be professional pretenders. We've become adept at putting on a facade, acting as if everything is fine even when we are hurt, broken, or suffering. This version of Christianity emphasizes appearances over authenticity, leading us to hide our true selves and struggles behind a mask of perfection. It teaches us to suppress our pain and avoid showing any signs of weakness, fearing judgment or rejection from others.

But this approach is fundamentally flawed. It denies the very essence of the gospel, which calls us to embrace vulnerability and authenticity. The gospel requires us to come before God and each other with our true selves, with all our wounds, doubts, and imperfections. It is in this raw honesty that the transformative power of grace can work in our lives. When we admit our brokenness and allow ourselves to be vulnerable, we create space for God's healing and restoration.

Pretending we are not hurt or broken isolates us from the genuine support and community we need. It perpetuates a cycle of loneliness and disconnection, as everyone is left feeling as though they are the only ones struggling. If we could break free from this cycle and be honest about our issues, we would discover that we are not alone. Vulnerability fosters genuine connections, empathy, and mutual support.

The gospel doesn't call us to project a flawless image; it calls us to be real. Jesus didn't die for the image we try to project; he died for who we truly are. He died for our authentic selves, with all our flaws and struggles. Embracing this truth liberates us from the need to pretend and opens us up to the profound work of grace in our lives. It's time to let go of the pretense and step into the freedom that comes from living authentically, knowing that we are loved and accepted just as we are.

As we consider this, let's focus our attention on a man named Jacob, who was *anything* but flawless.

Jacob was the son of Isaac and the grandson of Abraham, both towering figures in the annals of biblical history. Do you know what his name means? Jacob's name meant "deceiver." He was the younger of two twin boys, and he certainly lived up to his name. He deceived his brother, his father, and even himself. Jacob's life was a continuous struggle, a tumultuous journey through a landscape of deceit and ambition. Then one day he met a stranger.

Then Jacob was left alone; and a Man wrestled with him until the breaking of day. Now when He saw that He did not prevail against him, He touched the socket of his hip; and the socket of Jacob's hip was out of joint as He wrestled with him. And He said, "Let Me go, for the day breaks."

But he said, "I will not let You go unless You bless me!"

So He said to him, "What is your name?" (Genesis 32:24–27 NKJV)

This was a defining moment for Jacob, a pivotal turning point in the darkness of night. He was being asked the very question his Father asked him, "Who are you, my son?" (Genesis 27:18 NKJV) on the night he pretended to be his older brother, Esau, to receive the coveted birthright blessing from his father, Isaac. Up until this midnight moment he had never truly answered that question. Now Jacob was wrestling in the dark, his identity hidden amid the struggle. This was his opportunity to step out from the shadows and into the light of truth, settling this question once and for all. To ignite the fuse of authenticity that would lead to the demolition of every layer of deceit that coated his life. Would he own who he was, or would he again pose as someone else? Many of us face this same moment at some point in our lives, thinking about who we really are versus who we pretend to be. It's a moment when God asks, "What is your name? Who are you really?" Without hesitation, Jacob responded, "Jacob." Despite all the baggage and deceit associated with his name, he declared, "I am Jacob."

"And He said, 'Your name shall no longer be called Jacob, but Israel; for you have struggled with God and with men, and have prevailed'" (Genesis 32:28 NKJV). In a moment of truth and responsibility and accountability, a lifetime of pretending came tumbling down.

Once Jacob won the struggle within himself, he prevailed in his struggle with God. By being real with himself, he overcame the challenges posed by men.

Our spiritual health begins with our level of honesty about our struggles. You are only as spiritually healthy as you are honest.

The Scripture continues: "And He blessed him there" (v. 29 NKJV).

Jacob's blessing came from his breaking. From the moment God blessed Jacob and changed his name to Israel, he walked with a limp. Notice that when Jacob moved toward vulnerability, he was marked for greatness. Jacob's level of greatness was directly connected to the depth of his honesty and how willingly he shared it. As Paul said, "Therefore I will boast all the more gladly about my weaknesses, so that Christ's power may rest on me" (2 Corinthians 12:9). Boasting in our weakness only declares that much more about Christ's great strength working in us. It is not talent, intelligence, personality, or popularity that marks us for greatness. Our blessing comes in the same package as our brokenness. We are most useful to God when we are most honest about how he is redeeming us!

God never wastes a wound.

Our wounds are the windows through which the light of God's grace shines into the world. In our grief and brokenness, we can find comfort knowing that God is working through our pain to bring about his greater purpose. As an expression often attributed to Charles Spurgeon puts it, "I have learned to kiss the wave that throws me against the Rock of Ages."

Jacob named the place where he struggled with God "Peniel," saying, "For I have seen God face to face" (Genesis 32:30 NKJV). Face-to-face. No mask, no veneer, no pose— just transparency, honesty, and brokenness. Wrestling with God means being close to him.

Imagine Jacob standing there bruised and exhausted, with the dawn's first light revealing his battered form. His limp, a vivid reminder of his struggle, becomes a testament to his perseverance. Like a scar that tells a story of survival, Jacob's limp was a badge of honor, symbolizing his relentless pursuit of truth and his unwavering determination to confront his own identity.

In this profound encounter Jacob's transformation is not just a label but a declaration of his victory over deception and his embrace of a divinely ordained destiny.

As we reflect on Jacob's journey, we see that our own struggles are not in vain. Each challenge we face, each wound we endure is a brushstroke on the canvas of our lives, painting a picture of resilience and faith. In our darkest hours, when we wrestle with doubt and fear, we can find solace in knowing that God is with us, molding us through our trials. Sometimes being vulnerable about our grief or disappointments feels like we're wrestling with God in the dark, struggling to understand his purpose and seeking comfort in our pain. The joy in wrestling with God is that, in the wrestle, he holds us close. It is in these intimate, raw moments of struggle that we are transformed, and we emerge with a deeper understanding of ourselves and our place in his divine plan.

In our moments of mourning, we can, like Jacob, find comfort and strength. Our scars, both visible and hidden, are marks not of shame but of grace. They remind us that we have faced the storm and emerged stronger, more compassionate, and closer to God. Just as Jacob saw God face-to-face, we, too, can encounter him in our most vulnerable moments, being honest before him and experiencing his love and mercy in profound ways. We learn from Jacob that sometimes a truth bomb must precede a joy bomb.

My desire is that one day we will all be willing to step out of the dark, over the line from hopelessness to hope, from hurting to healing, from struggle to surrender—that we will look around the rooms of our lives, beneath the cross, seeing one another and hearing Jesus finish that statement: "If you really knew me, you'd know that you are not alone."

I'll be the first to admit that I've struggled with the idea of being vulnerable. I tend to project my best self—what I'd like to be noticed, known, and valued for. I've projected a certain image hoping to protect my insecurities. I always found a way to overstate my admirable qualities to shield my private flaws from the public view. The problem with all of that is this: The walls we use to protect our images are the same walls that imprison us with our pain.

I've dealt with considerable rejection in my life. I felt the inherent sting of rejection that came with being a kid caught in the middle of divorce. I felt the pain of rejection when several families left my wife's church over their shocking disapproval of our interracial marriage. I've had fellow Christians push me to the fringes of the denomination I grew up in, had them criticize me personally, had them scoff at the ministry that God was developing in me. And that was all before I turned twenty-four. And what was my response through all of this?

I performed so that I might be accepted.

We can all find ourselves in this position at one point or another. I don't know of many lives that rejection hasn't tarnished. Rejection was certainly a reality for Jesus. Scripture tells us that he was "the stone the builders rejected" (Matthew 21:42). The book of John says, "He came to His own, and His own did not receive Him" (1:11 NKJV). We see in the Gospels how his adoring fans became a vicious mob.

It's remarkable that Jesus remained unwilling to perform for acceptance. We see this in his temptation in the wilderness. The devil's strategy was to tempt Jesus to prove his identity through his ability to perform on command. The Enemy was essentially saying, "If you are the Son of God, prove it!" We are all met daily with a similar temptation, aren't we? "You have value, you're intelligent, you're beautiful? Prove it! Post it! Perform for acceptance!" But when we give in to the pressure to prove ourselves, we lose ourselves. Jesus didn't give in, and neither should we. Even when asked to do good things, he refused the Enemy, saying, "I only do what my Father commands."

Maybe you're asking the same question I asked myself: *How do I escape the pressure to perform and find the freedom in being real?*

I found the answer while considering an event that happened before Jesus had even performed his first miracle, the event that took place immediately before his temptation in the wilderness—his baptism. When Jesus was baptized, a voice spoke from the heavens, saying, "This is My beloved Son, in whom I am well pleased" (Matthew 3:17 NKJV). I believe that Jesus didn't feel the pressure to perform for the devil or for people because he knew that he was already pleasing to the Father.

And now maybe you're asking the same follow-up question I asked: If Jesus pleased the heart of God before he ever performed a miracle, why should we feel so much pressure to perform for God or anyone else? Who we are known by should trump that for which we are known. With God, we are not loved based on reputation; we are loved based on relationship. We can live beyond the approval of the world because we live from the affirmation of God.

What is the result? *Joy.* Marvel with me for a moment about this. I've found the real remedy for feelings of rejection, and it isn't in tirelessly performing but through receiving the work that Christ has already performed for me. It's through knowing that I don't have to project an image of perfection but that instead I get to take on the image of Christ. I don't have to mask my flaws either. Even the glorified body of Jesus had scars, so why would I attempt to hide mine with the superficial coverings of status, salary, or success? I've decided that the show is over. Now I get to live vulnerably before my Savior, in whom I am fully known and truly loved, accepted, and approved.

We can be filled with joy *and* still be grieving. We can grieve but not like those without hope. When we weep, the Comforter weeps with us. When we're broken, he's close. But instead of mourning, we try to manipulate ourselves or our circumstance to detach ourselves from our wounds rather than let God touch and heal them. We may be facing deep, deep sadness, but there is a deeper joy. Sometimes we can't get high enough to get over it. We have to be willing to go deep enough to get under it, where the springs of living water flow. Jesus saw in humanity that we would face these seasons of mourning. The wisdom of Solomon tells us that there is a time to mourn. So that time should not be avoided, because it gives way to the season of rejoicing. We give ourselves permission to deal with our pain. We give God permission to heal our pain and be our Comforter.

PERMISSION TO FEEL

Luke 12:7 tells us that God has numbered the hairs on our heads. God knows the sum of the hairs on your head, but he also has a number for each one! He knows that hairs #674, #223, and #62 came out in your comb this morning. He knows that #112, #332, #27, #96, and #705 are a little grayer than they used to be. It seems simple, but can you feel the full weight and reality of the truth of that verse? God sees, investigates, and keeps track of every single detail about his children. Not a freckle, scar, hurt, or moment of our lives is overlooked. Considering this truth, my heart echoes David's as he realized that the eyes of the Master were upon him. *Who am I that you are mindful of me?*

If God cares enough about you to number your hairs, do you think he cares enough to hear how you feel? This may not be a popular opinion in the religious sphere, but God is uniquely aware of and interested in your emotional life. He is interested in your highs, lows, ups, downs, breakups, breakdowns, and breakthroughs. Not only does he want to hear about your state of being from your lips to his ears through prayer and conversation, but he wants to surround you with a community of like-minded, caring friends of faith who give you the same permission to feel that he does.

I can't believe I'm admitting this, but my kids are now keeping me in touch with trends. I guess this happens to every parent at some point. I'm just in denial that the time has come for me! They are always teaching me new phrases, such as the meaning of "rizz" or how to use the phrase "ate and left no crumbs" correctly. They play me songs and music that resonate with the world. There are always a few phrases, influencers, artists, and songs that break through the noise to a place of prominence.

Back in 2018 a phrase caught fire: various forms of "in my feelings." If a person was "feeling a way" about something or in a difficult emotional place, that person was "in their feelings." This idea was carried on the sound waves of culture by Drake. "In My Feelings" was a number one smash hit song. It has now amassed 1.4 billion streams. This isn't a coincidence. Artists have a unique ability to interpret the world and express it through words and melodies. They help us make sense of our inner worlds. These songs become the soundtracks of our lives because we see ourselves in them. We find our experiences reflected in the lyrics and melodies.

A generation found itself connecting with the idea of accessing our emotions, for better or worse. Through this artistic expression people found permission to feel. Although Drake expressed it with catchy phrases, there's a deeper aspect to consider within the human soul when an idea resonates so widely. Why does the concept of being "in our feelings" connect on such a massive scale? It's because all of us, at some level, are trying to understand and manage our emotions.

For many of us who grew up in church, faith and feelings often seem like two separate categories. We might think that we must step out of our feelings to embrace our faith fully. If we want to feel our emotions, we might think we need to set our faith aside because it seems too hopeful or neat for the messy reality of our feelings. We need to reconcile these ideas of faith and feelings.

A few years ago I had a recurring conversation with my wife that went like this:

"Babe, everything okay?" she would ask.
I'd respond, "Yeah, I'm good." And then *silence*. I

preferred awkward silence over addressing my real emotions.

Eventually, we sat down with a pastor to talk through things. I realized that my surface-level symptoms were rooted in deeper issues. It took the work of the Holy Spirit to unravel these complexities. I have found we can use spiritual experiences to escape the real work we need to do on the inside. We can turn spirituality into a drug. That's what I did, at least. I didn't really want God to heal me; I wanted God to numb me. I had turned faith into a narcotic, relying on sermons, YouTube videos, and hyped church services to keep from going into my emotions and, more importantly, letting God in to perform surgery on my soul. But what I see now was that as I was holding myself back from negative feelings, I was also holding myself back from joy— joy within, and joy shared in connection with my wife. Perhaps this is a piece of what "blessed are those who mourn" means.

In church you'll often hear phrases such as "faith over feelings" or see these words on the back of a T-shirt. I understand the intention of this slogan, but it sends the wrong message— that faith is something we elevate while we bury our feelings beneath it. The problem with burying feelings is that we bury them alive. They aren't gone; they're just not visible. When we bury our feelings, we don't resolve them. Instead, they linger beneath the surface, affecting our thoughts and behaviors in ways we may not even realize. These unresolved emotions can manifest as stress, anxiety, or even physical ailments. Over time suppressed feelings can build up, leading to emotional outbursts or a sense of emotional numbness. The truth I want you to discover is that elevated levels of faith do not require suppressed emotions. No, real faith creates surrendered emotions.

"Faith over feelings" sounds like a good sermon on Sunday, but it doesn't help us navigate our emotions during the week. The sermons we hear can inspire and uplift us, urging us to place our trust in God more than anything else. But when Monday comes and we're back in the real world, dealing with our daily struggles, the disconnect between our faith and our feelings becomes apparent. We need to figure out how to integrate the gospel into our feelings to lead more holistic and authentic Christian lives.

Emotions influence every relationship in our lives. Whether it's the joy we share in moments of celebration or the pain we experience during conflicts, our emotions are a significant part of our human experience. Unresolved emotions, such as anger, jealousy, or grief, can hinder our connections with others. They can build walls that isolate us, even from those we love the most. Instead of avoiding emotions, we must allow the gospel to come alive in our emotions, bringing healing and transformation. We need to be a people willing to mourn if we want to be a people who will be comforted.

The gospel teaches us about love, forgiveness, and grace, but these principles often stay in our minds as intellectual concepts instead of becoming the guiding force in our emotional lives. By applying the gospel to our feelings, we can experience true freedom and peace. For instance, when we feel anger rising within us, we can remember the forgiveness we've received through Christ and choose to extend that for-giveness to others. When we are overwhelmed with anxiety, we can find comfort in God's promises, knowing that he is in control and cares for us.

Integrating the gospel into our emotions can strengthen our witness to others. People are drawn to authentic relation-ships and are often skeptical of those who appear to have it all together without acknowledging their struggles. By being open about our emotions and showing how the gospel helps us navigate them, we provide a powerful testimony of God's work in our lives. This authenticity can encourage others to explore their faith more deeply and find their own emotional healing through the gospel.

Ultimately, embracing our emotions through the lens of the gospel is not about disregarding our faith in favor of feelings but about harmonizing the two. It's about acknowledging that God created us as emotional beings and that he desires to meet us in those emotions. By doing so, we can live more inte-grated and fulfilling lives, where our faith and feelings are not at odds with each other but work together to bring us closer to God and to one another. We need to cry *together*. We need to laugh *together*. We really can't do one without the other.

THE JOY OF BEING KNOWN

Relational poverty is one of the greatest challenges our cul-ture faces today. These days we tend to have followers but not friends, likes but not love, comments but not conversations, crowds but not companions, churches but not communities. Our society has popularized a new kind of relational experience—one that gives us a broader network of contacts but lessens the importance of having meaningful connections with others. The priority on I, me, mine has eclipsed any sense of us, we, ours, and the result is that people feel more alone than ever before. Our time has been dubbed the "age of loneliness." In fact, it's estimated that one in five Americans suffer from chronic loneliness.[3]

Loneliness has a way of compounding. When we feel alone, we assume that we're the only ones who have ever felt that way. You might feel alone in the pain of a devastating loss, alone in your addiction, alone in your marriage. You might feel alone as a parent trying to raise kids, as a professional trying to balance your life, as a student struggling to find your identity. When we feel alone, we can start to feel unknown. And sometimes in those moments we feel the temptation to compromise who we are. Alone can be a dangerous place.

Eve had a conversation with the serpent; Noah got drunk; Moses committed murder; David destroyed Bathsheba and Uriah's life; Peter denied Jesus—and all of these things happened when these people were alone. There's a pattern here. This is why God said, "It is not good that man should be alone" (Genesis 2:18 NKJV). We were created for connection. We were created to be *known*.

I have tasted the bland reality of loneliness, and I have learned that the feeling of loneliness is an internal siren alerting the soul to the craving that we must be known by God and by other people. In that way loneliness can serve a purpose in our lives, at least initially, but there are only a few reasons—none of them good—as to why we might choose to perpetuate that stark existence. At the top of that list is love's opposite, apathy.

Apathy is indifference. It's the "I don't care" attitude that arrests our desire to love and be loved, leaving us coasting through life feeling alone and unknown. Our apathy serves as a coping mechanism that shields us from feeling. We secure ourselves behind the brick and mortar of statements such as "I don't care what people think about me," when, if we're being honest, the opposite is true. We care about what people think of us so much that we can't deal with the idea of letting someone know us—all our quirks, strengths, weaknesses, worldviews, gifts, and gaps—because that gives them the power to accept or reject us based on our level of vulnerability. So we create superficial selves and relegate every relationship to the shallow end of the relational experience. Because we know how badly rejection can hurt, we're afraid that someone might get to know us and decide not to like us. But the foundation of intimacy is vulnerability, and if we can't be vulnerable, honest, and open, then we will never be able to escape the terrible prison of superficiality. We will never be able to fully embrace what it is to be real.

John wrote that Jesus came to us in glory from the Father "full of grace and truth" (John 1:14).

I'm sure I could divide the readers of this book into two

groups: grace people and truth people. We have some people who prefer to view their world—their concept of God, the Bible, their faith, other people—through the lens of God's grace, and we have others who prefer to view these things through the lens of God's truth, which sheds light on our own sinfulness. When we rely too heavily on one of these lenses, when we prioritize one over the other, we are left with a distorted picture of reality. If we claim just one—grace *or* truth—without the other, at best we are in error. At worst we are denying who Jesus, who is full of grace *and* truth, really is.

Jim Collins, author of *Good to Great* and coauthor of *Built to Last*, coined the term "the genius of the AND."[4] He was using it in a business sense, but, in a broader sense, Jesus was the originator and embodiment of that principle. I've found that as believers we often love the dichotomy of either-or and struggle with the tension of both-and. We find ourselves gravitating toward the either-or passages in Scripture because we (especially truth people) like when there is a definite boundary between two categories. But Jesus defies categories. Jesus is the personification of the genius of the *and*.

All the fullness of the Godhead dwells bodily in Jesus. That means the Father and the Son and the Holy Spirit reside in him. Theologians (and we common folk) have struggled for centuries with the tension of that truth, and we have also struggled with the tension between grace and truth. Jesus was 100 percent full of grace and 100 percent full of truth. Everything hinges on that! A gospel without the truth of human sinfulness is meaningless, for what is there to be saved from if there is no truth to expose how we miss the mark? A gospel void of grace is powerless, for how can we be delivered from the truth of our sinfulness without the power of grace to set us free from it? We can't be heavy on truth and light on grace or heavy on grace and light on truth. Each option leaves us without the fullness of Jesus. With God it's hard truth, truth that exposes exactly who we are, and it's ridiculous grace, grace that meets us right where we are.

One of my favorite expressions of this grace-truth union is in the account of Jesus with the woman at the well. Because Jesus was full of grace, he wasn't afraid to break numerous customs of the day to reach her. She was a woman. She was of a different ethnicity. And Jesus had the audacity to tell this woman directly that she had a past riddled with sin. Then he followed that harsh truth by revealing himself as the Messiah, the one who takes away sin. He extended grace to her. This woman told her whole town what happened, and many people became believers. I love what it was that compelled her to believe. Her testimony was this: "He told me everything I ever did" (John 4:39). In other words, "He knew me." He knew the truth about her and didn't reject, condemn, or judge her. He showed her the love of the Savior.

I want to get better at being like Jesus, being able to step into the truth of people's lives and extend God's grace. I also want to get better at accepting the truth of my inadequacies and believing that God's grace is made perfect in my weakness. He knows us all and still loves us all. Understanding that, bringing it deep into your soul, will detonate a joy bomb in your life. Oh, the wonder of grace and truth!

HAPPY ARE THE INTENTIONALLY HUMBLE

Blessed are the meek, for they

will inherit the earth.

MATTHEW 5:5

DEBUNKING THE MYTHS OF MEEKNESS

Depending on how you look at it, I had either the fortunate or unfortunate experience of having my uncle and youth pastor as a teacher at my high school. Having a family member who's also your youth pastor working at your school definitely came with some unique pros and cons. It was easy to get an excused tardy note if I spent a bit too much time singing and socializing in the halls between classes, but I also couldn't get away with much either! But I had the chance to drop by his classroom during breaks or lunch, especially during my senior year. We called these visits "five-minute mentor time," and we'd dive into John Maxwell books and explore leadership principles. These moments became a catalyst for the rest of my life and ministry, as they instilled in me a love for the transformational knowledge one can gain from someone else's experience and expertise through a book.

That deposit of values is a big part of why you're holding this book in your hands (or listening to the audio version). This passion for reading eventually led me to discover other influential thinkers, such as a guy named Simon Sinek.

Simon Sinek is probably a name you've heard before, but if you're not familiar, Simon is a well-known author and communicator who broke out a few years ago with a book entitled *Start with Why: How Great Leaders Inspire Everyone to Take Action*. He encourages his readers to dig a bit into their motivations for careers, businesses, and projects. He asserts the notion that people don't just buy into what we do; they buy into why we do it, highlighting how much the motive matters.

Simon's message resonated with me. His words echo a fundamental truth: Our intentions shape our actions. When we understand our "why," it becomes a guiding star, helping us navigate through life's challenges and opportunities. It's like having a compass that always points north, reminding us of our true purpose.

Years ago a friend challenged me to find and define my "why." It's a good thing I did, because people often ask me why I do the things I do, whether it's making music, preaching, starting a new church, or even writing this book. The answer hasn't changed for me over the years. My "why" is to call greatness out of others. I want people to know that their story is possible, that God can use their lives, their wounds, and their talents to elevate his kingdom.

This journey of finding my "why" was transformative. It was a period of introspection and soul-searching that unveiled a profound desire within me: to inspire and uplift others. Each time I see someone realize their potential, it feels like a victory, a confirmation that we are all vessels of greatness, each with a unique role in God's grand narrative.

My guy LeBron James is undeniably good at basketball. His stature, athleticism, basketball IQ, and accomplishments irrefutably declare that he is special and one of the best to ever play the game. But there's this thing that LeBron continually does, with great intention. He frequently tells us that he is the greatest ever, that he deserves respect, and then tells us why. Of course, he's not the first, and he's not the only one. Muhammad Ali said, "I'm young, handsome, fast, pretty, and can't possibly be beat!"[1] Cristiano Ronaldo asserts that he's better than Lionel Messi.[2] Kanye has claimed to be a modern-day Walt Disney, Picasso, and Warren Buffett wrapped up in one person.[3] And the list goes on. These are just a few people who come to mind.

It's fascinating to observe these figures, their confidence sometimes bordering on arrogance. While their self-assurance is admirable, it raises an important question: Does greatness need constant self-promotion? Or is true greatness self-evident, shining through actions and achievements rather than declarations?

It's not just that sports, entertainment, and political cultures are littered with self-promoters; the human heart is a self-promotion machine. It's not just a LeBron issue or a Kanye issue; it's a me issue, and it's probably a you issue too. Especially if you're an entrepreneur, church planter, writer, coach, or salesperson. A big part of our job is to emphasize our distinctiveness to stand out in a crowd so that we get to add value to people's lives. We all want to be recognized, celebrated, credited, and admired to a certain degree. Most of us want to be great and excel at what we do. I know I do, and I believe—hot take—God wants us to be great too! Now, before you start quoting "the last shall be first" out of context and googling the verse that says "The greatest among you will be a servant" or, even worse, pinning me to a version of the prosperity doctrine that you loathe, give me a minute or fifty.

This desire for recognition is deeply ingrained in us. We yearn for validation, for someone to acknowledge our efforts and achievements. It's a universal longing that transcends cultures and professions. But in this pursuit we must remember that our worth is determined not by others' applause but by the intrinsic value bestowed upon us by our Creator.

Yes: God wants you to be great. For the sake of those whom that statement may rub the wrong way, let me pose a few questions. If God is inherently against human greatness, why would he tell Abraham that he would make his name great in the land and that a great nation would come out of him? If God is against success or notoriety in general, why would he tell Joshua, "I will elevate you in the eyes of the people" (3:7, author's paraphrase)? If God is opposed to humans doing great things, why would Jesus tell his disciples that they would "do even greater things than these" (John 14:12)? Why would he bless Solomon with great riches and grant prosperity to countless kings?

These questions are not rhetorical; they invite us to ponder the nature of greatness in God's eyes. The Bible is loaded with stories of individuals who achieved greatness, not for their glory, but for God's. Their success was a testament to his power and purpose, a beacon that illuminated his love and justice.

Don't we consider Paul the greatest missionary of all time or Billy Graham the greatest modern-day evangelist? Is that wrong? I don't want to make this turn too quickly, but perhaps the key is that *we* consider them to be great; they didn't. More about that in a few sections!

God's call to greatness isn't confined to ancient times. It's a living, breathing reality that continues to unfold in our lives today. People such as Paul and Billy Graham remind us that our lives can have a profound impact, rippling through generations.

Personally, I don't have a problem giving titles of greatness to athletes, actors, artists, professors, preschool teachers, or paramedics. Because here's what I know: Even at the ultimate height of human success, greatness, or achievement, God is unrivaled in glory. It's a fool's errand to even attempt to put our accomplishments in any category that relates to the greatness of God. He is other. He is categorically in a category of his own—perfect, holy, unmatched in strength, and unparalleled in power. That's clear. But I also want you to understand that God wants you to be great. A great man or woman, student or professor, husband, father, daughter, friend, photographer, athlete, worker, writer, employee, or business owner. As Scripture tells us, "Whatever your hand finds to do, do it with all your might" (Ecclesiastes 9:10). You were destined for it. But let me be clear: This greatness is not defined by cultural norms of wealth, fame, or followers.

This understanding of greatness is liberating. It means that our value is measured not by external success but by our faithfulness to God's call. Each role we play, no matter how small it may seem, is significant in God's grand design. Your everyday actions, when done with love and dedication, echo in eternity.

Tony Evans defined greatness with striking clarity and simplicity in his book *Kingdom Man*: "Greatness is maximizing your potential for the glory of God and the good of others."[4]

Evans's definition brings us back to the heart of the matter. Greatness is not about self-aggrandizement or bravado; it's about serving others and glorifying God. It's about using our gifts to make a positive impact, to be a light in the darkness, and to inspire others to discover their own potential.

If you've been waiting for permission to be great, here it is: You were created on purpose for a purpose. You were created by love for love. You were created by greatness for greatness. Your past mistakes and triumphs, your present struggles and strengths will be used by God when they are surrendered to God. You have permission to throw off the fear, insecurity, or doubt that holds you back. You have permission to become all that God has called you to be. It starts today. It starts right now.

It's time to ignite this truth in your soul: Your life is a masterpiece in progress. Each experience, whether joyful or painful, is a brushstroke on the canvas of your destiny. God, the Master Artist, is crafting something beautiful out of your existence, something that will resonate with his glory and love.

You may be thinking, *Well, how could I be great for God? What could I do, what could I offer?* And you'd be in good company, asking the same questions as Abraham and Sarah when God called greatness out of them, telling them that they'd give birth to a nation as countless as the stars. "Us? We haven't been able to have one child, and those days are over." Or Moses when God called greatness out of him. He had his reasons why he couldn't become great. Or maybe you feel like Noah, who accomplished one of the greatest feats in human history when he constructed the ark. No one called it great or recognized his achievement in his time. He received quite the opposite. How about Gideon? God called him great while he was hiding out and trying not to be seen. What about David, who wasn't even invited into the house to be considered for king? Fast-forward to Mary, an obscure teenager tucked away in anonymity, who became the mother of God. Mind blown. People even overlooked the greatness in Jesus, so don't be surprised if they don't see what God has placed in you.

God does.

These biblical stories remind us that God often calls the unlikely, the overlooked, and the underestimated. Your perceived limitations are no match for God's limitless power. He sees potential where others see none. He calls forth greatness from the most unexpected places.

Here's a truth bomb: Being more visible doesn't make you great. It just makes you more visible.

Visibility can be fleeting, but true greatness endures. It's not about how many people see you but how deeply you touch those you encounter. It's about the legacy you leave behind, the lives you change, and the love you spread.

Being famous doesn't make you great.

Not everyone famous is great, and not everyone great is famous.

Fame is a double-edged sword. It can bring admiration but also scrutiny. True greatness is quiet and humble, thriving in the shadows where it's nurtured by sincerity and integrity. It's about the substance of your character, not the spotlight on your stage.

Being wealthy doesn't make you great. Money doesn't make an individual; it only reveals what's already there.

Wealth can amplify your influence, but it doesn't define your worth. It's a tool that can be used for good or evil. True greatness uses resources to uplift others, create opportunities, and sow seeds into the dreams of others.

Being accomplished doesn't make you great. You can excel in one category and fail in another. That's not what true greatness really looks like.

Accomplishments are milestones, not measuring sticks. True greatness lies in your resilience, kindness, and unwavering commitment to your values. It's about who you are, not just what you do.

God is not calling you to be great by the world's standards; he's calling you to be great by his. God's standards are different from the world's. They are rooted in love, humility, and service. They call us to look beyond ourselves, see the divine in every person we meet, and act with compassion and justice.

Let's excavate that layer deeper.

One of my biggest pet peeves in sports is postgame interviews where athletes just tell you about how amazing they are. This is rampant in bravado culture. You see, in the process of becoming all that God has created you to be, you will not have to tell anyone how awesome you are—*they* will tell *you*. If you're a leader, you won't have to tell anyone—people will just follow you. If you're wise, you won't have to tell anyone—people will listen to you. Now, I'm not against marketing, strategies, and Instagram posts that allow people to discover the value you can add to their lives with your gifts, insights, and expertise. There is a stewardship component here that's important as well. Just ask the man who buried his talents how that worked out for him.

The point is, your greatness will speak for itself. It will be evident in the lives you touch and the impact you make. Steward your gifts wisely, share them generously, and trust that God will amplify your efforts in his perfect timing.

At dinner the other night, our friends were sharing the humble beginnings of their now-remarkable hospitality tech company. It started as just a side hustle helping one hotel get its IT systems flowing properly. My friend did great work. The word spread about him, and supporting one hotel turned into eight, and eight turned into twenty-two, and now, only five years later, twenty-two has become thousands with zero marketing. They didn't have to tell people they were great; the right people realized it at the right time, and God elevated their business.

This story is a testament to the power of excellence and work ethic. When we focus on doing our best and serving others, recognition follows naturally. It's a beautiful reminder that God's favor often comes in unexpected ways, blessing our efforts when we least expect it.

With four boys, my wife and I find ourselves at a lot of flag-football fields, basketball gyms, and baseball diamonds. I love watching my kids play sports—maybe a little too much, but God is working on me about that! There's an attitude and a swagger that kids have these days. It existed when I was a kid, for sure, but we didn't have the same language they have now. After a young athlete snags a football from over an opponent's head, the boys yell, "Head top!" Or if they make a great defensive play, they make a motion that looks like they're buckling a seat belt, as if to say, "I strapped 'em up." But what takes the cake is when, after a strong move to the hoop or a step-back three, they yell, "*I'm him!*" I can't lie; I love the confidence and the passion, but this isn't a mindset of humility.

God does more in and through us when we humble ourselves, not when we hype ourselves. When you declare "*He's him!*" when you humble yourself, Scripture says, God will exalt you. The Scripture even says those who exalt themselves will be abased or brought low. You see, joy isn't found at the heights of our aspirations or the pinnacle of our achievements. No, I've discovered that Jesus places his greatest gifts on the bottom shelf, where only those willing to humble themselves can reach them. Remember, God doesn't oppose greatness, but he does oppose the proud. Those who sing their own praises soon discover the crowd has left. Proverbs says it like this: "Let someone else praise you, and not your own mouth; an outsider, and not your own lips" (27:2).

Humility is a powerful force. It attracts grace and opens doors that pride would slam shut. When we choose humility, we align ourselves with God's heart. He lifts us up, not for our glory, but for his. True greatness is rooted in knowing who we are in God and letting him work through us. Individuals who are truly great are usually unaware of it because they have this quality that is produced by the Spirit of God: the quality of being meek.

GENTLENESS AND JESUS

Meek.

When was the last time you ascribed that word to someone? For some of you, the only reference point you have for "meek" is a rapper from Philly. If you don't know who I'm talking about, skip that last sentence and don't think twice about it! In a culture that has a cele-hate relationship (celebrate-hate relationship . . . you like that, huh?) with those who are bold and brazen, outspoken and ostentatious, extreme and just plain extra, "meek" is not a word we use very often, is it? It's not a word that we would drop into the bio lines of our IG or LinkedIn pages to elevate our social profiles. Not only is it a rare description of someone in the culture, but it's unfortunately a rare description of believers! I've heard Christ followers called a lot of things and described in a lot of ways and I could count on one hand how many times the word "meek" has been the descriptor of choice. We live in a fast-paced world where assertiveness is celebrated. People who exhibit meekness might be viewed as being pushovers or lacking in self-confidence, which is a gross misinterpretation of what it means to be meek. There are two prime examples of people in the Bible who mastered meekness—Moses and Jesus—and neither of them was a pushover. Particularly Jesus.

Much has been said about Jesus, written about Jesus, debated about Jesus, claimed about Jesus, sung about Jesus, and thought about Jesus. The Scripture shares thirty-seven miracles of Jesus; he is described by almost two hundred names or titles in the Scriptures. There are endless libraries written about his life, his passion, and his heart, yet there is only one instance in the four gospels when we hear from Jesus's own lips how he describes his own heart . . . and he describes it like this: "Come to me, all you who are weary and burdened, and I will give you rest. Take my yoke upon you and learn from me, for I am gentle and humble in heart, and you will find rest for your souls. For my yoke is easy and my burden is light" (Matthew 11:28–30).

I am gentle and humble in heart.

Gentle.

Humble.

The Son of God, the one in whom the fullness of the Godhead dwelled, the Christ, described himself as meek.

When Jesus spoke of his heart, he was not merely

referencing his emotional life. When the Bible uses "heart," it transcends our emotional life and means the very center of who we are, the force that drives us, the central animating center of all we do. So when Jesus described what drove him, it was not power or prestige, dreams or goals, or even joy and abundance—it was meekness.

Now, don't get me wrong—Jesus was not weak. We often carry the misconception that meekness is weakness. Meekness can be defined simply as strength under control. It's really no surprise that meek people are happy, joyful people. The meek are not driven by the acquisition of power, appetite for authority, or attention of admirers. The meek are given claim to the earth because their humility proves that they can handle it. Jesus was the embodiment and personification of meekness.

Being meek doesn't mean you must conceal your strength; it just means you carry the humility to reveal your weaknesses. This concept is exemplified in the life of Jesus. He was well acquainted with his strengths, and he never shied away from acknowledging them. After all, he was crucified for telling the people that he was God—a bold claim by any measure.

Jesus's strength was not just in his divine identity but in his connection and obedience to the Father. He openly declared his divinity, performing miracles, forgiving sins, and teaching with authority that amazed and sometimes infuriated those around him. His confidence in his identity and mission was unwavering. But Jesus consistently pointed back to his source of power and authority.

In John 5:19, Jesus said, "Very truly I tell you, the Son can do nothing by himself; he can do only what he sees his Father doing, because whatever the Father does the Son also does." This statement underscores a significant aspect of meekness: the acknowledgment that our abilities and strengths are not self-generated but are gifts or powers granted by God.

In John 14:10, Jesus reiterated this dependence: "Don't you believe that I am in the Father, and that the Father is in me? The words I say to you I do not speak on my own authority. Rather, it is the Father, living in me, who is doing his work." Here Jesus emphasized that his words and actions were in perfect alignment with God's will. He did not operate independently but was in constant communion with the Father, doing only what he was directed to do. His meekness was displayed in absolute surrender to the will and purposes of God.

This humility did not diminish his strength but rather amplified it. It cast a bright light on a profound blend of power and submission, authority and humility. Jesus highlighted the divine nature of his mission and the power that backed it and yet did not use his power for himself but for his purpose to serve and save.

In practical terms, being meek and humble means recognizing and openly admitting that our talents, skills, and strengths are not merely products of our efforts but are given and sustained by something greater. It means understanding and living out the truth that our strength lies in our reliance on and obedience to God.

This approach completely changes how we look at and

use our strengths. Instead of using power to promote self or eclipse others, we focus on serving others, guided by God's purpose. Just like Jesus, who used his divine strength to heal, teach, and ultimately sacrifice himself for humanity, we're called to use our strengths to benefit others. Our abilities are gifts to be shared, not personal assets to be hoarded.

Meekness, then, is about having an active and dynamic humility. It's the strength to recognize where our abilities come from and the wisdom to use them for the right reasons. By doing this, we not only reach our true potential but also honor the divine origin of our strengths, just as Jesus did.

STRENGTH AND STATUS

I once had a mentor who said, "Strength is for service, not for status." That always stuck with me, and it's perfectly shown in the life of Jesus.

Jesus really lived this out when he said, "The greatest among you will be your servant" (Matthew 23:11). He didn't just talk the talk; he walked the walk by washing his disciples' feet, one of the humblest acts recorded in the Gospels. Even though he was the King of kings, he didn't try to elevate himself above others. Instead, he lowered himself to serve, showing that true greatness comes from humility and service to others.

And here's something even more profound: Jesus, being divine, didn't cling to his equality with God. Philippians 2:6–8 says, "Who, being in very nature God, did not consider equality with God something to be used to his own advantage; rather, he made himself nothing by taking the very nature of a servant, being made in human likeness. And being found in appearance as a man, he humbled himself by becoming obedient to death—even death on a cross!" This highlights Jesus's ultimate commitment to humility. Despite his divine nature, he chose to live among us, experience human limitations, and sacrifice himself for our salvation.

Jesus's decision to become human and his sacrifice on the cross are the ultimate acts of humility and service. They show that true strength isn't about asserting dominance but about selflessly valuing others above yourself. By following Jesus's example, we learn that our strengths and abilities should benefit others; in this way we reflect the same humility and service that Jesus showed throughout his life.

Jesus's life and teachings give us a clear guide on how to use our strengths. We're called to serve rather than be served, to give rather than receive, and to humble ourselves rather than exalt ourselves. By doing so, we fulfill our true potential and honor the divine source of our strengths.

My wife is a huge action-film fan, and although I'm more of a romantic-comedy guy myself, our family's preferences converged around watching the entire Marvel movie series as a family (with VidAngel to filter any questionable content, of course). The boys loved the superhero-studded movie marathon!

One iconic scene stood out, and you probably remember it if you've seen it. This scene takes place in *Avengers: Age of Ultron* when the Avengers are enjoying some downtime at Tony Stark's luxurious penthouse. The mood is light and relaxed, a respite from their usual high-stakes battles. The team is gathered around, laughing and bantering, when Thor's hammer, Mjolnir, becomes the center of attention. The mystical weapon, engraved with the inscription "Whosoever holds this hammer, if he be worthy, shall possess the power of Thor," rests on a coffee table. Tony Stark, ever the curious and competitive genius, suggests a friendly contest to see who among them can lift it.

Tony Stark, also known as Iron Man, is the first to take up the challenge. He saunters over, his confidence unshaken, and grasps the handle of Mjolnir with a smirk. Despite his considerable strength and the assistance of his Iron Man gauntlet, the hammer remains immovable. He jokes about how it must be a trick, but deep down he knows it's more than just a game.

Next up is Bruce Banner, the man behind the Hulk. Bruce hesitates, knowing that his alter ego's brute strength is unparalleled, but his own human form is much less formidable. He tries it, to no avail; the hammer stays put. The team chuckles, but there's an undercurrent of seriousness as they all wonder what it means to be "worthy."

Then Steve Rogers, also known as Captain America, steps forward. His demeanor is humble, and he approaches the challenge with a quiet resolve. As he grips Mjolnir, there's a moment when it seems to budge ever so slightly, causing Thor to look on with a hint of concern. But the hammer doesn't lift, and Steve steps back with a modest smile.

The attempt by each hero to lift Mjolnir is more than just a display of strength; it's a revealing moment about their characters. Thor, the only one who can wield it effortlessly, explains that the hammer's enchantment requires worthiness, a trait defined by integrity, honor, and selflessness . . . meekness.

No one was deemed worthy to handle the immense power, so no one could lift it. In this context, meekness isn't about weakness but about humility, integrity, and selflessness—qualities that the mighty Avengers, despite their physical prowess, must embody to be truly humble.

This is the takeaway: It wasn't a lack of physical strength that limited what they could carry; it was an absence of pure motives and the mastery of will. It wasn't possible to lift the weapon with the strength of their bodies; they had to lift it with the strength of their character. Some things can never be accomplished merely by great strength, but only through *pure* strength. Meekness is a purity of strength. Strength can be corrupted by status, but it is supercharged by service.

The meek don't promote themselves but rather rally around the gifts of others.

The meek realize that strength is for service, not for status.

The meek intentionally wire their lives in connection to the joy of the Lord because they are aware that their strength, though God-given, is a finite resource and is dependent on the breath of God. When God breathes on something, there's no denying the wind!

I know I'm a lot happier, filled with more joy, when I remind myself that while God allows me to be part of his plans, my power in producing outcomes is limited. God is the one who promotes, advances, and elevates. He opens doors, and he closes them. God owes me nothing, so everything I receive is a gift. This perspective keeps me grounded and reminds me of the divine grace that flows into my life, unearned and undeserved. That is the mindset of the meek, believing that the way up is down. This means embracing humility and recognizing that progress comes from a place of surrender, not force. Hustle, manipulation, and a strong hand might force movement temporarily, but such tactics are short-lived and often lead to stress and burnout. On the other hand, humility, self-control, and patience allow God to move supernaturally in our lives. These virtues create a space for divine intervention, where God's timing and wisdom surpass our limited understanding.

This code is about finding a healthy balance between our own efforts and trusting that God is ultimately in control. Whether you're a college student juggling classes and exams, a single mom balancing work and family, or someone between jobs looking for new opportunities, it can feel as though everything depends on you. But while it's essential to put in effort and take steps forward, it's also freeing to realize that you don't have to have it all figured out. Sometimes, no matter how hard we try, there are things beyond our control. Embracing both action and surrender helps us avoid burnout and allows space for God to work in our lives. Instead of feeling pressured to handle everything on our own, we can trust that God's timing and provision will lead us to the right opportunities and the support we need.

If the general definition of meekness is "strength under control," I would add a spiritual layer to it and say, "I want strength under God's control." This means not just controlling my strength but surrendering it to God's guidance. It's about trusting that he knows the best path for me even when I don't see it. This kind of strength is not about overcoming weakness; it's about channeling our abilities into alignment with God's will. When we are determined to grab everything we can for ourselves, we limit God's ability to give us everything we can't get on our own. Our self-driven pursuits can create barriers to our receiving God's blessings, which are far greater than anything we could achieve through our efforts. By letting go and trusting in God's provision, we open ourselves to lives of a joy-filled abundance that goes beyond material success and taps into spiritual fulfillment and peace. This shift from self-reliance to divine reliance transforms our approach to life, making room for miraculous changes and profound contentment.

THE HARD TRUTH ABOUT SOFT POWER

Considering everything we have investigated on the subject so far, it's not that surprising that it will be the meek who inherit the earth. It seems as if the things of the world are usually attained through acquisition and dominance, and that may be true in some ways for now. But the meek will conquer with kindness, acquire through consideration, and lead with love. Meekness produces its own core qualities such as patience, gentleness, and kindness, which evoke trust. And God hands what is precious to him to people he can trust.

Why can the meek be trusted? Because when their patience is tested, they pass the test. When their kindness seems illogical, they can't think of operating in any other way. When their gentleness is misunderstood, they find an even softer touch. They can be trusted with everything the earth brings, governing with grace from the overflow of joy. The meek know how to drop joy bombs that devastate pride and clear the way for God's power.

As a new pastor one of my key responsibilities is to help create a church culture that honors God and others. This often begins with empowering church leaders with the proper framework for how we relate to one another.

Recently I came across a podcast featuring an incredible philosopher, designer, and pastor, Erwin McManus, along with his son, Aaron McManus, a brilliant creative and thinker in his own right. In one episode they discuss the concepts of hard power and soft power. They articulate that hard power involves the use of force and directness to drive results within a relationship or culture. It is a command-oriented way of communicating. In contrast, soft power is an approach that uses more finesse and emotional awareness in communicating and giving directives.

One insightful analogy from the podcast was about keeping children safe on one side of the street. Erwin explains that sometimes, even if children do not understand the philosophical reasons behind certain rules, hard power must be used to protect them and provide clarity of instruction and must be acted upon immediately. As they state, "Sometimes you have to use hard power to protect people and to bring clarity and to bring continuity in an organization."[5]

But they also emphasize that hard power should not become the core of an organization. "When hard power becomes the body, there's no flesh, there's no warmth, there's no life to it."[6] A healthy culture within a team, family, or organization should be 10 percent hard power and 90 percent soft power. This highlights the importance of balancing hard power with soft power to create a nurturing and effective environment.

SOFT POWER VS. HARD POWER: A SIMPLE ANALOGY

When you think about the pace of the slowest person versus the fastest, remember two key things about power:

1. Soft power (meekness) doesn't make you weak; it makes you influential.
2. Hard power isn't always the fastest way to get things done.

Let's use a cool physics experiment to explain this.

THE PHYSICS EXPERIMENT: BALLS AND TRACKS

Imagine an experiment with two tracks and two balls.[7] Each ball starts at the same point, but the tracks are different:

TRACK 1: A straight line
TRACK 2: A slightly angled line

You'd think the ball on the straight track would finish first, right? Surprisingly, the ball on the slightly angled track gets to the end faster. Why? Because the angle gives it some extra momentum, even though it travels a bit farther.

Here's how the experiment relates to power:

HARD POWER (STRAIGHT LINE): Like the straight line, hard power aims to get results quickly by force. It's direct but doesn't build momentum.

SOFT POWER (ANGLED LINE): Like the angled line, soft power takes a bit longer at first. But it gains momentum through cooperation and agreement, getting things done faster with more relational equity invested.

Using soft power is like building up speed on a downhill slope. At first it might seem slow, but as you gain more agreement and cooperation, you pick up speed and move faster toward your goal. Hard power, on the other hand, is like pushing straight ahead without gaining that extra momentum.

By taking the time to build relationships and get people on your side, you can often achieve your goals faster and more effectively than by trying to force your way through.

This discussion on power dynamics ties directly into the biblical principle of meekness. When you operate with strength under control, you use your power, strengths, and gifts appropriately and wisely, not for domination or division, but for the benefit of others. Practicing meekness involves a deliberate choice to respond with gentleness and humility, even when one has the power to do otherwise. Meekness is the essence of soft power; it is about leading with grace, influencing through compassion, and achieving lasting results through humility.

I had our team watch the podcast, and over the course of the next several weeks we tagged our statements as either hard power or soft power. This exercise provided a great template for practicing meekness, helping us to be more aware of how we communicate and lead. By distinguishing between hard and soft power, we learned to embody meekness, ensuring that our actions and words are guided by gentleness and respect, reflecting the love and grace of God in our church culture. Our leaders and "vision owners" are grasping this as more than just a concept—it's a way of being. And do you know what? There is extraordinary joy in our meetings and gatherings, because there is great joy in the life of the meek.

CODE FOUR

HAPPY ARE THE INSATIABLY HUNGRY

Blessed are those who hunger and thirst
for righteousness, for they will be filled.

MATTHEW 5:6

CONSUMED BY YOUR CRAVINGS

It's time for me to make a confession, fam. My name is Tauren Wells, and I love candy. Yup. I said it. Candy. I know, I know, a lot of people prefer a great dessert, such as molten chocolate cake or bananas Foster. But not me. No, I don't get down with a lot of desserts, but don't get it twisted for even a second—I have a sweet tooth! I love Hot Tamales and sour Mike and Ikes, Almond Joys, and a cold Snickers during a round of golf. I must also admit that every year I splurge and venture outside of the candy aisle during Girl Scout cookie season. I just have to support one of my nieces or a young girl in our church by buying an unreasonable amount of peanut butter chocolate cookies. It's the right thing to do! Hey, let me tell you something: Those peanut butter chocolate cookies are undefeated right out of the fridge as a late-night snack. Whew!

Now, I know I'm supposed to avoid sugar to stay healthy, but because of the way sugar works, the more candy and cookies I have, the more candy and cookies I crave. It's a vicious cycle! After a few days of crushing the sweets, I'll notice that I'm slow, grumpy, foggy, and inflamed. My mood tanks, my energy plummets, and my brain feels like it's running in slow motion. But do you know what I want? More candy! It's as though my body's stuck on a sugar treadmill that just won't stop. To break free from this prison somewhere in candy land, I must deny myself these unhealthy cravings through fasting and then start consuming the right things. It's tough at first, but once I start eating better, my energy levels rise, my mood improves, and my mind clears up.

See, our appetites drive our attitudes. This is true both spiritually and practically. For years nutritionists have noted that poor food choices create poor attitudes in adults and children. How we feel is directly affected by how we fuel ourselves. Think about it: When you fuel with junk, you feel like junk.

When we consistently consume unhealthy foods, our bodies respond negatively. We experience sluggishness, mood swings, and a general sense of malaise. On the other hand, when we choose nourishing foods, our energy levels stabilize, our moods improve, and we feel more capable of tackling the day's challenges. This principle extends beyond just physical nutrition.

One of my favorite books is *Atomic Habits* by James Clear. It's a game changer, and you should read it . . . right after you finish this one. Clear gives us a deeper general insight into this process. He shares that every habit has a feedback loop:[1]

CUE > CRAVING > RESPONSE > REWARD

Clear states, "Cravings . . . are the motivational force behind every habit. . . . What you crave is not the habit itself but the change in state it delivers. . . . Every craving is linked to a desire to change your internal state."[2] For instance, you might not crave the act of eating a candy bar, but you crave the temporary boost in energy and mood it provides. This craving drives your response—eating the candy—which then gives you the reward of that desired change in state, completing the feedback loop.

Let's delve into each component of this loop to better understand how habits form and how they can be changed.

1. **CUE:** The cue is the trigger that initiates the habit. It can be a time of day, an emotional state, a specific place, or the presence of certain people. For example, stress after a long day at work might serve as a cue to reach for a sugary snack.

2. **CRAVING:** The craving is the motivational force behind the habit. It's the desire to change your internal state. When the cue is present (e.g., stress), it creates a craving for relief or comfort, which you associate with a specific habit (e.g., eating a candy bar).

3. **RESPONSE:** The response is the habit you perform, which can be a thought or an action. This is your behavior in reaction to the craving. If you crave a sugar rush to alleviate stress, your response might be to grab a candy bar from the pantry.

4. **REWARD:** The reward is the end goal of the habit. It's the satisfaction and relief you get from the craving. This reward teaches your brain that the habit loop is worth remembering in the future. Eating the candy provides a temporary mood boost, reinforcing the habit loop.[3]

I know that we have used something as simple as a candy craving as an example, but there are many things we might reach for in different situations when we try to meet a spiritual or emotional need with something material and temporary. It could be infinity scrolling on social media, binge-watching Netflix, compulsive online shopping, or even using substances. You can fill in the blank and apply this understanding where it's appropriate. But by understanding this principle of the feedback loop, you can be empowered to make better choices. By recognizing your cues and cravings, you can intentionally alter your responses to create healthier habits.

Clear's research highlights that to change a habit we must disrupt the feedback loop at any stage. One approach is to modify the cue by making it less obvious or avoiding it altogether. For instance, if you want to stop eating junk food when you're stressed, you might remove unhealthy snacks from your home and replace them with healthier options. For several years Lorna and I and our boys have done a fast to start our new year. Lorna and I basically eat grass and drink hot almond milk (if you close your eyes it tastes like coffee . . . kinda). But the boys fast sugar. To even make this remotely possible, we throw away anything with even a gram of sugar in it because if it's there, we are no match! But when we align our surroundings with our aspirations, we create a strategy to succeed.

Another method Clear leads us to is to change the craving. This involves associating the cue with a different craving that leads to a healthier response. Instead of craving a candy bar for comfort, you might train yourself to crave a quick exercise routine or a few minutes of meditation, which also alleviate stress but in a healthier way.

Altering the response and reward can significantly aid in habit formation. Instead of reaching for a fourth cup of coffee, opting for a healthier alternative such as a smoothie or a piece of fruit can still satisfy the craving while promoting better health. Over time, your brain begins to associate this new response with a positive reward, reinforcing the healthier habit. By understanding what you're truly craving, you gain the power to satisfy yourself with things that genuinely fulfill you. There is a spiritual principle for this: "Do not be conformed to this world, but be transformed by the renewing of your mind" (Romans 12:2 NKJV). Paul was saying that we ought not be tethered mindlessly to the ways of our culture in a general sense. But I believe it also applies to not mindlessly conforming to patterns, behaviors, and environments that we continue to repeat and exist within that are not healthy or holy and certainly don't detonate Jesus's joy in our lives. An essential part of renewing your mind is reconstructing your environment.

There is no real distinction between your everyday life and your spiritual life because all of life is spiritual. But your spiritual life is lived out *practically*. Therefore, incorporating positive practices and healthy rhythms is essential in every area of life. The more you hunger for righteousness, the more you will be filled with righteousness. This principle applies to various spiritual disciplines as well. For instance, the more I give, the more I desire to give, and soon generosity becomes second nature. Similarly, the more I study Scripture, the deeper I want to dive into it; and the more I pray, the stronger my connection with God becomes. These spiritual practices create a hunger for more of the same. The more I consume righteousness, the more I crave it. These practices bring me into God's presence, where there is fullness of joy.

Psalm 16:11 says, "You make known to me the path of life; you will fill me with joy in your presence, with eternal pleasures at your right hand." This verse highlights the joy and satisfaction that come from being in God's presence. Do you want to be filled? Filled with the joy of the Lord? Develop an appetite for his presence, and you'll never be empty a day in your life.

The truth is that whatever we crave consistently, we will be consumed by eventually. If you hunger and thirst for money, you will find a way to get it. If you hunger and thirst for power, you'll find a way to become influential. If you hunger and thirst for fame, you'll find a way to get a following. If you hunger and thirst for pleasure, you'll have all the fun you want.

Here's the issue: Money, power, fame, and pleasure can get you a lot, but what they are powerless to do is satisfy your soul. Proverbs 27:20 says, "Death and Destruction are never satisfied, and neither are human eyes." They leave you always wanting more, never truly fulfilled. Desiring God, on the other hand, satisfies the desires in me. Psalm 37:4 encourages us to "take delight in the Lord, and he will give you the desires of your heart." It fills the deepest parts of my soul that nothing else can reach. So if you want to live a life of true satisfaction, start by developing an appetite for his presence. Trust me, you'll never be empty again.

I was sitting in my songwriting room at my house about a year ago thinking about the amazing fact that I have a room in my home that Lorna let me decorate any way I wanted (major win). This room is exclusively a space for me to let my creative juices flow. It is a stark contrast from the "creative spaces" I used to write and record in for two decades, like in closets or under a blanket at the dining room table. I took a long look around the room admiring my deep green walls that held several plaques serving as memorial stones of songs that, by the grace of God, have connected with people all over the world. What a blessing!

I could hear the busy little feet of three of my boys on their latest adventure through the upstairs. Probably in ninja costumes, with flashlights and all types of makeshift weapons as they hunted make-believe monsters. What an incredible blessing! In the other room my amazing wife was prepping the house for our family that would soon gather to celebrate an award ceremony that was on TV, in which I had the privilege of being featured. It's the dream! What a blessing!

I went over to the upright piano, the same piano I started the song "Hills and Valleys" on just a few years back. With all the good that surrounded me and with all the beauty that filled my life, I thought when my hands touched the keys, a song of gratitude and praise would burst out. But the words that flowed over a simple melancholy chord progression were "You could have it all . . . and still feel empty." Was my life full but my soul empty? If it was, I wasn't aware of what was happening beneath the surface, in my soul. If it were true, how could I feel this way? Here I was, surrounded by more than I could ever need or deserve—a beautiful family, a flourishing ministry and career—but still an intangible longing persisted.

I sat there, fingers hovering over the keys, pondering this strange feeling. It wasn't that I was ungrateful for the blessings in my life. I knew I was incredibly fortunate. But why, despite all of this, did I feel an emptiness gnawing at me? I started to dig deeper into this paradox, searching for answers.

Solomon, whom most credit as the gatherer and distributor of the wisdom of Ecclesiastes, was the wisest man who ever lived. He was also one of the wealthiest and most revered and successful people in all of history. He shared the often-overlooked truth that God has placed eternity in our hearts (Ecclesiastes 3:11). A universe-sized expanse that would swallow the world whole if it could—and still be hungry. Wow! What a remarkable insight that helps us clarify the feelings that so often rise to the surface even when things are going well and our dreams are coming true. Even if something is good, even if something is a blessing, even if something is a gift from the very hand of God, it's still not God and is therefore unable to quench the thirst for what we crave most.

Reflecting on Solomon's wisdom, I realized that my soul was longing for something deeper, something eternal. That material blessings didn't equate to a matured contentment, and a full schedule didn't equate to a full soul. That various achievements, as wonderful as they are, can never fully satisfy the ache within our hearts for the residence of God's presence. They can bring temporary joy and fulfillment, but they cannot fill the eternal void placed in our hearts by God. This void can be filled only by an active and vibrant relationship with him.

A friend of mine recently sent me the book *40/40 Vision: Clarifying Your Mission in Midlife*, and I have been spending a lot of time with it. In their commentary on purpose in life, the coauthors, Peter Greer and Greg Lafferty, share two profound perspectives that made me reevaluate my life in a whole new light.

"You have to face the meaninglessness of your self-made life before you can find meaning from another source."[4] This resonated deeply with me. We too often get caught up in constructing lives based on our own achievements, possessions, and societal standards of success.

Greer and Lafferty further quote Georges Bernanos, whose words struck me profoundly: "In order to be prepared to hope in what does not deceive, we must first lose hope in everything that deceives."[5] This quote underscores the importance of letting go of false hopes and illusions. It is a call to recognize and relinquish the superficial and deceptive sources of fulfillment we often chase. Like a person who must delete his digital clutter to find clarity and peace, we, too, must let go of the things that deceive us to find hope.

In a world full of distractions and misleading promises, it's easy to place our hopes in things that ultimately let us down. Bernanos's insight reminds us that hope and purpose can be found only in what is genuine and enduring. This process of losing hope in what deceives can be painful, as it requires us to confront uncomfortable truths about our lives and choices. But it is a necessary step toward finding a more authentic and satisfying source of hope and meaning.

In my writing room that day, I was challenged to examine my life critically and to seek a deeper, more substantial foundation for my hopes and dreams. To shift my focus from the temporary and unreliable to the eternal and steadfast.

It is a resetting of expectations. I realized the need to ask myself more questions about the motives behind the expectations that I set. I'm a goal-oriented person. I love setting and achieving goals. I don't want to waste my life or anything great or small God gave me to fulfill his purpose for my life. I think that's good, but I'm trying to readjust what I am expecting to receive from the things that I want to accomplish. I know, as I'm sure you know, that only God can satisfy the soul. So I have to ask, *What am I really expecting from my wife, from my kids, from my job, from my ministry, from my advancement, from my life on earth?* If I'm expecting them to give me what only God can, well, I'll always feel empty.

I started to see that my expectations were often misaligned from a deeper spiritual reality. I expected my achievements to bring me ultimate satisfaction. I expected my family to fill every void in my heart for happiness. I expected success in my ministry to affirm and complete me. These are all wonderful things, but they are not designed to fulfill the deepest longings of the human soul. That job belongs to God alone, and he is jealous for it.

Matthew 5:6 says, "Blessed are those who hunger and thirst for righteousness, for they will be filled." This verse became a guiding light for me. It reminded me that satisfaction comes from seeking God and his righteousness. The more I focused on my relationship with God, the more my soul felt full. It wasn't that the blessings in my life became any less significant, but they found their proper place in my heart.

I began to prioritize my time with God, making sure that I was seeking him first in everything. I spent more time in prayer, more time reading the Bible, and more time simply being in his presence. And as I did, the emptiness faded. My soul was being filled with the joy and contentment that only God can provide.

In John 4:13–14, Jesus spoke to the woman at the well and said, "Everyone who drinks this water will be thirsty again, but whoever drinks the water I give them will never thirst. Indeed, the water I give them will become in them a spring of water welling up to eternal life." I realized that I had been drinking from the wrong wells, looking for fulfillment in places that could never satisfy.

The more I sought God, the more I understood what it meant to be truly fulfilled. It wasn't about having more things or achieving more success. It was about being in a right relationship with God and finding my identity and purpose in him. This was a key shift in my thinking, and it brought a new sense of peace and contentment to my life.

I also started to notice how my changing attitude affected those around me. My family could see the difference in me. I was more patient, more loving, and more present. My ministry was affected as well. People could sense the authenticity and depth in my messages. They could see that I wasn't just talking about God's love and fulfillment—I was living in it.

Imagine the transformation that God could bring if you sought fulfillment in him rather than in achievements or in the endless striving to attain. What would your life look like if your identity and purpose were rooted in God's love and grace? How might this shift fill you with a unyielding sense of peace and contentment, rippling outward like a joy bomb and touching everyone around you with the love of Christ? Would your family, friends, and coworkers notice the change in your heart and attitude—overflowing now with God's patience, love, and presence? By allowing God to work through you, how might you be sharing his joy wherever you go, inspiring others to experience the same in their own lives? Could embracing this transformation be an invitation to become a vessel of God's love, revealing his grace through your quiet contentment and radiating bursts of joy that reflect his divine presence?

I can't answer these questions for you, but I can say that this journey has been transformative for me. It's not that I have everything figured out or that I never struggle with feelings of emptiness anymore. But I have learned where to turn when those feelings arise. I have learned to seek God first and to trust that he will fill me with everything I need.

An even greater truth to acknowledge is that we will never feel ultimate fulfillment or satisfaction here on earth. I know. That can be frustrating in a way, but that soul ache is a persistent reminder that one day we will inherit heaven. One day, as we step onto that golden shore, we will breathe deeply in relief that our souls finally have everything they've always wanted.

As C. S. Lewis wrote in *Mere Christianity*, "If I find in myself a desire which no experience in this world can satisfy, the most probable explanation is that I was made for another world."[6] This world is not our final home, and our ultimate satisfaction will be found in the presence of God in eternity. Until then, we can find joy and peace in our relationship with him, knowing that he is the source of all true fulfillment.

So if you find yourself feeling empty despite the blessings in your life, I encourage you to seek God first. Spend time in his presence, read his Word, and pray. Ask him to fill the void in your heart and help you find your satisfaction in him. As you do, you will unlock joy that only he can provide. And you will be reminded that, no matter how full your life may seem, only God can truly fill your soul.

Your appetite for God may be insatiable, but no matter how deep your desire is to draw from the well of God's goodness, his ability to fulfill you is infinitely greater. He never runs out of that which satisfies! Who can know the unsearchable riches of God? His love, grace, and mercy are boundless, far beyond our comprehension. As we seek him, we discover that his provision and blessings are endless, constantly surpassing our greatest expectations. In God's infinite wisdom and generosity, he continuously pours out his goodness, ensuring that our spiritual hunger is always met with an abundance that overflows. As Ephesians 3:8 says, "Though I am the least deserving of all God's people, he graciously gave me the privilege of telling the Gentiles about the endless treasures available to them in Christ" (NLT).

PLANTING SEEDS OF PROMISE

Most nights our bedtime routine with the boys is a special mix of fun and faith. As time allows, we'll read a book together, sing a few songs, and, if I'm on duty that evening, have a little dance party (against their mother's wishes, of course!). There are nights when we have less time than others, but we always, always pray. Sometimes we invite them to pray as well, giving them the chance to speak to God in their own words.

When they first started praying, they would always begin with "I hope . . ." At first I almost corrected them, thinking there was a more "proper" way to pray. But then I realized they might actually understand prayer better than I did. They were starting their prayers with hope, and I saw something beautiful in that.

Every great prayer starts with great hope. Faith is the substance of things hoped for, the evidence of things not seen. This means that the prerequisite to prayer is faith, and the prerequisite to faith is hope. The truth is, you won't pray if you don't have faith, and you won't have faith if you don't first have hope.

Hope is how faith writes checks. Against all odds, "against

all hope, Abraham in hope believed and so became the father of many nations" (Romans 4:18). The father of faith was, at his core, a man with hope. Hope is the first ingredient you need for a miracle!

"The Kingdom of Heaven is like a mustard seed planted in a field. It is the smallest of all seeds, but it becomes the largest of garden plants; it grows into a tree, and birds come and make nests in its branches" (Matthew 13:31–32 NLT).

Show me a praying person, and I'll show you a person full of faith!

The prayers we pray say a lot about the faith we possess. It takes faith to pray. Faith is the foundation on which we build our knowledge of the reality of God. Faith is the currency of heaven, and prayer is how we exchange sorrow for joy, ashes for beauty, and spiritual deadness for supernatural power.

When we attempt to fulfill ourselves by placing our faith in anything other than God, we always come up empty. Instead of praying and receiving the joy of the Lord as an outflow of our relationship with Jesus, we try to purchase joy and peace by other means. Life becomes one social escapade after another—buying as much stuff as our credit card limit will allow, hanging out with friend after friend after friend, filling our lives with shallow relationships and meaningless things—and all the while true joy and real peace and genuine companionship and lasting satisfaction are waiting to be found in an intimate relationship with Jesus, a relationship that is initiated and sustained by faith.

Jesus spoke of faith as a "mustard seed." In this parable

about the mustard seed, Jesus was sharing an important idea with us: Faith begins in seed form. Faith in God is planted in the soil of our hearts and cultivated by the Spirit of God, and, over time, it produces joy, peace, humility, fulfillment, power, and every other rich quality of the character of God. Faith is the source of these blessings, and prayer is the way that the source gets into the soil.

Some people do not feel inclined to pray because often-times prayer just looks like a seed. Nothing too thrilling or filling about a seed, right? But through the eyes of faith, we don't just see our prayers for what they are when we're praying them; we see the potential of what they can become when God answers them. Great prayer reveals great faith, and great faith releases great prayers. Great faith is measured not in magnitude but in our resoluteness to believe God against all odds.

So let's talk a bit more about prayer and joy. Do you know how sometimes life feels heavy and dull? Maybe you're stuck in a rut, doing the same old things, or maybe you're feeling the weight of stress and worries. That's where prayer comes in. It's like a direct line to God, a chance to unload all your concerns and find a fresh perspective.

When you pray, you're not talking to the ceiling; you're connecting with the Creator of the universe. Think about that for a second! It's like having a heart-to-heart with someone who understands you completely and loves you unconditionally. When you lay your burdens down in prayer, you make room for joy to enter. It's a joy that doesn't depend on circumstances but comes from knowing that God is in control and has good plans for you. Prayer is the action of people who are hungry and thirsty for Jesus.

Prayer isn't always about asking for things either. It's also about gratitude and thanksgiving. When you start counting your blessings and thanking God for the good things in your life, no matter how small, something amazing happens. Your focus shifts from what's wrong to what's right, and that shift brings a sense of joy and peace that's hard to explain but so wonderful to experience.

So if you want more joy in your life, make prayer a habit. It doesn't have to be long or complicated. Just start talking to God as you would a close friend. Share your heart, listen for his voice, and watch how your faith grows and your joy multiplies. It's a journey worth taking, and the best part is that you're never alone on this journey. God is with you every step of the way, ready to turn your prayers into joy, one small mustard seed of faith at a time.

This brings us to another powerful scripture: "Those who sow with tears will reap with songs of joy" (Psalm 126:5). This verse is a beautiful reminder that even in our hardest times, when we feel broken and weary, our tears are not wasted. Think about it this way: Shedding tears in times of sorrow is like watering the seeds of faith we've planted.

When you're going through tough times and you feel like all you can do is cry, remember that these tears are not for nothing. They're part of the process. God sees every tear and understands every pain. In those moments of sorrow, when you turn to God in prayer, you're sowing seeds. It's as though you're saying, "God, I don't understand why this is happening, but I trust you. I'm giving this to you."

Over time these seeds will grow. The Bible promises that those who sow in tears will reap in joy. It means that your moments of deep pain will eventually lead to moments of great joy. It's a transformation that God brings about, turning our mourning into dancing, our sorrow into gladness. This joy is profound because it's born out of trust and faith in God, and from knowing that he is with us and working everything for our good.

If joy is a spiritual resource, it is produced from a spiritual seed: prayer. Just as a gardener plants seeds expecting a harvest, our prayers are seeds planted in the spiritual realm in expectation of a harvest of joy. When we pray, we are planting seeds of faith. These seeds might not look like much at first, just like tiny mustard seeds, but with time and the right conditions they grow into something magnificent.

Imagine a garden where each prayer you make is a seed planted in the soil. You water it with your faith, nurture it with trust in God's timing, and, eventually, you see the first sprouts of joy emerge. It's a process that requires patience and persistence, but the results are worth it. The joy that blooms from these seeds of prayer is not fleeting or shallow. It is deep-rooted and resilient, able to withstand the storms of life because it is grounded in the steadfast love and promises of God.

The next time you find yourself overwhelmed with tears, remember this promise. Turn to God in prayer, pour out your heart, and trust that he is using even your tears to grow something beautiful in your life. The joy that will come from this will be deep and lasting, a testament to the power of faith and the goodness of God.

When you feel joy, it's not a fleeting emotion but a lasting sense of contentment and peace. This kind of happiness doesn't just happen; it's cultivated through a relationship with God. When you plant the seed of prayer, you are actively participating in God's plan for your life. You're inviting him into your circumstances, trusting him with your deepest concerns, and allowing him to work in ways you can't even imagine.

Prayer is like planting a mustard seed of faith in the fertile soil of God's promises. It might seem small and insignificant at first, but as it grows, it transforms your life, bringing forth an abundant harvest of joy. This joy is a spiritual resource that sustains you, uplifts you, and empowers you to face life's challenges with a hopeful and confident heart. So keep planting those seeds of prayer, and watch as God brings forth a beautiful, joyful harvest in your life.

HAPPY ARE THE UNREASONABLY FORGIVING

Blessed are the merciful, for
they will be shown mercy.

MATTHEW 5:7

JUMPING TO A BETTER CONCLUSION

I'm grateful that my kids have amazing grandparents. Grandparents seem to have a unique perspective on their grandchildren. It's as if grandchildren can do no wrong in their grandparents' eyes. If a child throws a fit, the grandparent will rush in with an explanation: "He must be tired." If he hollers and screams in an outburst: "He must need some attention." When she sneaks snacks from the pantry, it's "Well, I'm sure she was starving." They always give these little ones the benefit of the doubt. They're charitable in their thoughts toward them. They see the best, find the best, and choose to believe the best about them. It's not that they ignore wrongdoing or tolerate poor behavior; they are just instinctively empathetic and extend themselves to great lengths to try to understand the nuances of a choice, a behavior, or something that was said. Before jumping to conclusions, they jump to compassion. Before considering worst-case scenarios, they give the benefit of the doubt.

I need to learn from them. The biggest point of application for me personally is commenting on other people's thoughts, opinions, and actions that I see on social media. I know I've been completely misunderstood before, so I try to remain charitable in my thoughts of others when something doesn't seem clear to me. Before choosing judgment, I try to choose mercy. I choose to consider that there's a backstory I'm unaware of, a circumstance I can't see, or something else I may be missing. This is a small act of mercy, but when I sow seeds of mercy, I reap seeds of mercy in my own life. And what joy it brings to receive mercy when you deserve the contrary. This perspective creates joy. I'm joyful because I'm believing the best about others, and I'm joyful because this means God is choosing to believe the best about me!

In Luke 6:38, Jesus lit the fuse to an explosive spiritual reality. He said, "Give, and it will be given to you. A good measure, pressed down, shaken together and running over, will be poured into your lap. For with the measure you use, it will be measured to you."

So many times we downgrade this scripture to merely a passage about finances and generosity, an end-of-the-year offering, or a special purchase for a stranger during the holidays. But if we consider the rest of the context—loving our enemies, acting compassionately, and withholding judgment—we see that Jesus was calling his followers beyond their tax-deductible offerings and Venmo donations into opening their lives to others in an unreasonably favorable, empathetic, and thoughtful way. To be generous in grace, generous in forgiveness, generous in judgment. He was illuminating the reality of the reciprocity of generosity.

He was saying if you give judgment, you'll get judgment back, pressed down, shaken together, and running over. So make sure you judge the way you'd want to be judged! Give condemnation, and you'll get condemnation pressed down, shaken together, and running over! But if you give grace, kindness, and forgiveness to an unreasonable measure, you're going to get it back even beyond the extent to which you extended it!

To follow the words of Jesus, you must start by being generous with your life, your judgments, and your attitudes toward others. This commitment should spark a flame of joy within you. When forgiveness, compassion, and gracious words flow from you, you open space for the joy of Jesus to fill you!

Forgive others when they cross a line of offense with you, remembering that Jesus crossed the ultimate line of offense for you. Reflect on the overwhelming compassion God has shown you, and you'll be moved to show compassion to others. Ultimately, living in light of what your Savior has done for you inspires you to extend those same gifts to others—and this is a powerful path to experiencing true joy.

THE SECRET SOURCE OF SECOND CHANCES

Have you ever just really blown it? Well, I've got some good news and some *really* good news. The good news is that you're not the only one. And the really good news is that God's not done with you. In the middle of our failures, weaknesses, and struggles, we feel the true weight of God's grace, mercy, and love. If you're struggling and have been dealing with personal issues, heart trauma, or difficult situations, you're in good company, because everyone in human history has done the same. Let's take off the veneer of Christianity—all the shiny plastic social trappings that imply things such as "I'm so good. I never do anything wrong. I never struggle because I follow Jesus, and Jesus's followers don't struggle!" Ha! Yeah right! In fact, there's an extensive list of people who demonstrate that if you haven't failed yet, you will.

Abraham, the father of faith, lied. Elijah, one of the Bible's greatest prophets, was suicidal. Moses murdered someone. Gideon was consistently fearful. Samson broke his covenant with God. Rahab was a prostitute. The Samaritan woman was divorced and sleeping around. Noah got drunk. Jacob lied, over and over. Jonah rebelled against God's call and was extremely prejudiced. Martha worried—a lot! Zacchaeus stole tons of money from people. Paul killed Christians. And let's not even get started on the original disciples; they were all different flavors of dysfunctional. We all struggle. We all fall. We all fail. We are all merely human.

I want you to know that you are not the only one grappling with feelings of deficiency and the reality of sin. But here's the truth: Nothing can separate you from the love of Christ (Romans 8:38–39). No matter how low you may feel, Jesus can forgive you, restore you, and even use you for his glory.

I want to zoom in on the disciple Peter. Specifically, I want us to walk together through Peter's big (yet seemingly small) mistakes that culminated in the worst moment of his life. Spoiler alert: Peter denied Jesus. He didn't do it just once. He denied him three times. Now, you've got to look at Peter's highlight reel. This guy was selected as one of the original twelve disciples—a true OG. That's a big deal. He journeyed with Jesus—Mr. God on Earth himself—for three years. He had seen and been a part of tons of miracles. One of the writers of the Bible said that if he wrote down all the things that Jesus did, he wouldn't be able to capture it all, and yet Peter had a front-row seat to all of it! He was at the Last Supper, the very last time Jesus ever broke bread with people before being crucified. Peter was in the room with Jesus. Jesus himself told Peter that God was going to use him to build his church. In fact, Jesus renamed Peter. Simon was his given name, and Jesus renamed him Peter. If that's not a highlight reel, I don't know what is! But even with that pedigree and after all of that time with Jesus, all the moments when he encountered the glory of God, Peter messed . . . it . . . up.

We should never think that exposure to God equals immunity from sin. We can attend conferences, camps, retreats, services, and all kinds of religious gatherings, we can even be in dedicated service to the causes of Christ, and still be susceptible to spiritual sabotage. Sometimes we are so entrenched in church stuff that we skip the basic stuff that our lives with Jesus are built upon.

I think I've been guilty of moving too quickly through the sequence of events that preceded Peter's downfall. I often jump from Peter's bold declaration—"Even if I have to die with you, I will never deny you!" (Matthew 26:35 NLT)—to the rooster crow that signaled his first denial; however, our mistakes don't just happen all at once. Let's look closer at the events that led up to this moment in Peter's life. What if it wasn't Peter's weakness that led him to failure but rather his strengths?

Many of us are well acquainted with our weaknesses. We know the things that we lean into when we are not healthy, but we don't really consider our strengths as places where we can fall short and miss the mark. One of Peter's strengths was his bold personality. I think that's part of the reason Jesus called Peter in the first place—because he could take charge, move quickly, act with passion, and do the things Jesus called him to do without reservation. Jesus wanted this kind of personality on his team. The problem was that Peter never learned how to put guardrails on his gift. He never learned how to guard his strength, and an unguarded strength is a double weakness. Nothing can get you into more trouble than your strengths.

Are you a people person? Do you thrive off the energy of other people? If this strength goes unguarded, you could find yourself thriving not only on the energy of others but also on the acceptance of others, compromising values and beliefs to fit in with whoever is "in" at the moment.

Maybe you have a leadership gift and a mind for strategy and vision. What a gift! But if that strength goes unguarded, you may find yourself manipulating people and situations to execute your own agenda rather than championing others' skills, contributions, and gifts. Then you become a leader with blurry ethical lines, and your unguarded strength becomes a double weakness.

Perhaps you're good with money. You could be so good with money that soon all you think about is money—how you can get more, how you can save more. If this goes unguarded, you begin to hoard it instead of giving it, and now you are greedy and not generous. Any strength we have that is not surrendered to Jesus can be used as a weapon against ourselves and others.

We must guard our strengths. Because Peter was unwilling to accept the possibility of falling down, he was unprepared for his opportunity to stand up. When we admit that we are prone to failure, that our strengths aren't strong enough to save us, we find the power to live righteously through Christ.

Scripture says to take heed when you stand, lest you fall (1 Corinthians 10:12). When sin affects our opportunities to use our strengths, a perfect situation can become a perfectly wrong situation. Have you assessed your strengths lately?

The next thing Peter did seems insignificant in the grand scheme of things. He skipped the prayer meeting. After Peter declared his wholehearted loyalty to Jesus, telling him that he would die by his side if he had to, Jesus asked something so simple of Peter. He asked him to pray with him. But when Jesus came back, Peter was asleep. Jesus asked him to pray again, and again Peter decided that his time would be better spent catching some z's. How could Peter have the fortitude to die for Jesus if he couldn't even pray with Jesus? It makes me wonder: How many times do we make big declarations of faith but then fail to take the small steps of obedience that lead us to the fulfillment of those declarations?

"Stay awake and pray that you may not come into the time of trial; the spirit indeed is willing, but the flesh is weak," Jesus said (Matthew 26:41 NRSVue). *Pray that you're not led into temptation, Peter.* This was the warning. This was the moment that would have prepared Peter's lips with a resounding "Yes!" for when, in just a few hours, he would find himself sitting around a campfire being asked "Are you with Jesus?" This was the moment—the moment that would have prepared him for the greatest battle he would ever fight within his soul. It was a moment that no one would celebrate. It was a moment that no one would like on Instagram. It was a moment that he'd get no credit for. It was a moment that no one would ever see. I wonder whether it even would've been written in the Bible at all if Peter had just prayed with Jesus; surely they had all prayed together before, but we don't see it in Scripture.

Peter decided to sleep rather than pray, and he left his spirit unguarded. Prayer is the protective force around our lives. It positions us in a place of power. We should never underestimate the power of prayer. Yes, we pray for the needs of others. Yes, we pray for the needs of the world, but this was the moment for Peter to pray not for the world but for himself and to take inventory of his own heart—to follow the example of Jesus, who was in a garden praying so hard that his body produced blood out of his sweat glands. Yet Peter was asleep with his spirit unguarded.

We must get into that place of prayer. We've got to fight for that place of prayer and connection with Jesus. I'm not saying this in a religious way. I'm not saying this legalistically. Prayer is a relational imperative in the life of the believer. Sometimes we view prayer as a test for our discipline, but prayer is more than that. It is an indicator of the health of our relationship with God. Any relationship that exists without communication is unhealthy. Prayer guards our spirits. Prayer is a secret place, an uncelebrated place, at times a painful place, but it is a crucial place.

After this, Jesus was captured. Judas had just betrayed him. The officials were walking Jesus back to the house of the high priest and, the Bible says, "Peter followed him at a distance" (Matthew 26:58). We are all prone to follow Jesus at a distance.

I'm not convinced that Peter did this intentionally. Indeed, there are some who choose to follow Jesus at a distance because of what getting close may cost them, but most of us fall away from Christ one gradual step at a time. We think things such as *I don't need to go to church every Sunday; it's more of a tradition than a necessity. I don't need to get too caught up in worship; singing and lifting my hands doesn't really jibe with my personality. I know I haven't read my Bible in a while, but isn't having to read it just going through the motions anyway?* There are thousands of reasons we could give to explain away the gap between our hearts and God's presence. We fall away casually and gradually, never instantly. Scripture says, "Your word is a lamp to my feet and a light to my path" (Psalm 119:105 NKJV). We must watch our steps. We must make an intentional decision to pursue Jesus every day.

Christianity is lived on an incline, and if we're not moving forward, we're slipping backward. What's creating space between you and Jesus? Is it a friend group? A relationship? The strain and stress of your job? Your education goals? I've realized that the nobler the cause, the more we justify our distance from the cross.

We, on our own, are no match for the devil. We need Jesus. We do have power, but we access his power through proximity. We access his power by intentionally moving our hearts closer to him.

When someone is severely injured, it's often the case that he or she needs to be stabilized before being moved. Moving the person could cause more damage. In our spiritual lives the principle is the same. There are times when we fall that we need to stay down before we get back up.

After his epic failure we find Peter around a charcoal fire with people asking him, "Hey, do you associate yourself with Jesus?" He was like, "Nah . . . Wait, did you say 'Jesus'? 'Cause I did know a Jesus back in fourth grade, but *Jesus* of, like, Nazareth? No, I've never really heard that name before." After denying Jesus three times, he heard the rooster crow. He must've thought to himself, *Nooooooo! I just did exactly what I said I would never do.*

Matthew 26:75 says it all: Peter "wept bitterly." When you fall, stay down—down in a place of repentance, down in a place, on your knees, where you are contrite, broken, and sorrowful over the mistakes and the sin that have existed for too long in your life. Find an altar. It can be in your bedroom, at your kitchen table, behind the steering wheel of your car. Get yourself into a place where you are sorrowful about the wrong that has been done in your life. Weep bitterly.

The only way to overcome a failure is to walk straight through it. When we fall and when we mess up, we cannot just push all the broken pieces into the corner of the room and step out and pretend to be fine, acclimating ourselves to our dysfunction. We must have a Psalm 51 moment that echoes the cry of David: "Create in me a clean heart, O God. Renew a loyal spirit within me" (v. 10 NLT). Repentance cannot be overlooked. It is a crucial recurring theme in the life of the believer. This is what Jesus told Peter to do prior to his denials. He said, "I have prayed for you, Simon, that your faith may not fail. And when you have turned back, strengthen your brothers" (Luke 22:32). To repent means to turn around. When we fail, we confess it, for we have the power to conquer only what we confess.

Could the joy you're looking for be found on the other side of the prayers you haven't prayed? Could the peace you seek be waiting on the other side of the sins you haven't yet repented? There is a levity that comes from confessing our sins and experiencing the forgiveness that flows from the rich grace of God's goodness. When we hold back from prayer or repentance, we hold on to burdens we were never meant to carry.

Imagine what it would feel like to let go of those hidden regrets, those heavy sins, and allow God to lift them off your shoulders. Joy is often found on the other side of surrender—where we've turned over our fears, struggles, and brokenness to him. There is an incredible freedom that comes from repentance, a lightness in the soul that comes only when we let go and let God take control. The grace that God pours out when we bring our sins and struggles to him has the power to transform our hearts. When we are humbly surrendered to him, his joy, peace, and forgiveness flow into our hearts, filling them with the weightlessness of his love and goodness.

My friend Nick Nilson says, "Following Jesus for the long haul isn't about not falling down; it's about getting good at getting back up!" This is true. Failure is written in pencil. When we fall, and we stay down for a moment to repent and reflect. And when we are released by God, we get right back up. Get up today! You can't wallow in your shame forever. You can't walk around feeling guilty forever. Arise.

JESUS CANCELED CANCEL CULTURE

Our culture is quick to cancel anyone with a checkered past, neglecting the fact that everyone has fallen short of the glory of God. But God does not operate within the confines of cancel culture; he came to establish restoration culture.

Cancel culture is when people get publicly lambasted for something they've done or said that others find offensive or wrong. It can happen fast and hit hard. One moment someone might be a popular figure, and the next he or she is facing massive backlash. This usually involves a lot of public shaming. People lose job opportunities, endorsements, and even friends. Social media plays a huge role here—a tweet or post can go viral in minutes, spreading the criticism everywhere.

One of the biggest issues with cancel culture is that it often skips over any kind of fair process. Accusations are taken at face value, and there's rarely a chance for the person to explain or make amends. It's a lot of "guilty until proven innocent" but without the proving part. This can lead to serious mental health issues for those on the receiving end—anxiety, depression, and a feeling of being completely overwhelmed are common reactions.

The whole situation creates a big divide among people. Some think cancel culture is necessary to hold powerful individuals accountable, while others believe it's gone too far and shuts down open conversation and growth.

On the flip side, there's a biblical principle, established by Jesus, in which the merciful receive mercy; it's called "restoration culture," and it takes a very different approach. Instead of focusing on punishment, it emphasizes forgiveness and the chance for redemption. It's about understanding that everyone makes mistakes and that people can change.

In restoration culture, when people mess up, the goal isn't to destroy their lives but to help them learn and grow from their mistakes. It's about giving people a second chance. Forgiveness is key here—it's about letting go of past wrongs and supporting one another in becoming better. This culture believes in holding people accountable but doing so with compassion and a desire to see them improve.

Throughout the Bible there are countless stories of people who messed up but were given another shot by God. Peter wasn't the only person to make a mistake or commit the sin of denying Jesus. Take Paul, for instance. He was known for persecuting Christians, but after his dramatic encounter with Jesus, he became one of the most influential apostles. God didn't cancel Paul for his past; instead, he restored him and used him for a greater purpose.

Jesus himself emphasized forgiveness and restoration. He spent time with sinners, offering them a path to redemption rather than condemnation. The story of the prodigal son is a perfect example—the wayward son is welcomed back with open arms by his father, symbolizing God's unconditional love and readiness to forgive.

Restoration often takes place in the context of community. The Bible encourages believers to bear one another's burdens (Galatians 6:2) and forgive as they have been forgiven (Colossians 3:13). Instead of "canceling" the erring, we're to help them get back on their feet spiritually. It's all about the belief that no one is beyond redemption and everyone deserves the opportunity to make things right.

While cancel culture focuses on quick judgment and exclusion, restoration culture promotes healing, forgiveness, and the possibility of new beginnings. It's a reminder that everyone deserves a chance to grow and be better, just as God offers each of us grace and the chance to start anew.

The Bible records that a few women went to the tomb after the crucifixion and burial of Jesus and saw that he was no longer there. An angel said to the women, "Jesus is going to meet his disciples in Galilee. Go, tell the disciples and Peter" (Mark 16:7, author's paraphrase). He singled out Peter. Why? Because he wanted it to be clear that Peter was still a part of his plan. I can feel the essence of God's message in those two simple words *and Peter*. It's as if he was shouting, "Peter, I know you blew it. I know you messed up, but I'm not done with you. I want you to meet me somewhere, and if you're going to get there, you can't stay here. So get up on your feet in the grace and the power and the love that I just died for you to have and get moving. Get back up." Somebody reading this needs to hear that today. Get back up. So you fell down. "The righteous fall seven times" and "they rise again" (Proverbs 24:16). The righteous fall? The righteous fall. The righteous? That's the best of us, the cream of the crop, those on the top shelf. We fall, but we get back up. Get up standing in the righteousness of Jesus. Then get back to what you were called to do, because who you have been called to be hasn't changed. If you've made a mistake but repented, I've got good news: You're forgiven! So get up. Scripture says that when the women came to tell the disciples that the tomb was empty, all the disciples stayed seated, but Peter got up and ran to the tomb to see it for himself. If Peter could get back up, so can you.

When we flip forward to the book of Acts, we see Peter in Acts 1 devoting himself to prayer. It seems as though he learned the crucial need for a guarded prayer life. He's leading the group, choosing more disciples. He didn't just get back up; he got busy doing what he was created to do. Peter was not canceled by God; he was called by God, so Peter checked himself back into the game.

I have a question for you if you're feeling disqualified: Who disqualified you? Who canceled you? Who took you out of the game and put you on the bench? Jesus? I don't think so.

The voices of guilt and shame will whisper in your mind to convince you that your calling has been canceled. They will attempt to sow seeds of doubt, telling you, "They'll never listen to you again. You have no real authority. No one will trust you." But let me tell you—every one of those thoughts is dead wrong. Jesus has your back. He's fighting for you, and his love and support are unwavering.

David said, "Surely goodness and mercy shall follow me all the days of my life" (Psalm 23:6 NKJV). This means not just on the good days, the days when we get everything right and make no mistakes, but every single day. On your worst days, when you feel like you've failed beyond repair, God's goodness and mercy are still with you. They are your constant companions, lifting you up, guiding you, and reminding you of your worth and purpose.

So shake off those feelings of unworthiness. Get back to what God has called you to do. Remember, his mercy is new every morning. Every day is a fresh start, a new opportunity to walk in your purpose and live out your calling. God's plans for you are bigger than your mistakes. His love is stronger than your fears.

Imagine the impact you can have when you embrace this truth. You are defined not by your past but by the love and calling of God. Step into your day with confidence, knowing that you are chosen, loved, and equipped. The world needs your gifts, your voice, and your passion. Don't let the whispers of guilt and shame hold you back. Stand tall, embrace your calling, and move forward with the assurance that God is with you every step of the way.

You are more than your mistakes. You are a child of God, called to make a difference, and empowered to do great things. So rise up, take courage, and get busy with the work God has set before you. His grace is sufficient for you, and his power is made perfect in your weakness. Go forth with boldness, knowing that you are never alone and that each day brings new mercies and opportunities to fulfill your God-given purpose.

Have you ever been at one of those meals where it's a little awkward because you and your friends or family are sitting there with an elephant in the room? Everyone knows there's "a thing," but no one is talking about "the thing." In John 21, the disciples had been reunited with Jesus after his resurrection, and we find Jesus, Peter, and some of the others eating breakfast together. The Scripture seems to imply that they ate the whole breakfast without talking about "the thing." The tension is palpable.

When they had finished eating, Jesus said to Simon Peter, "Simon son of John, do you love me more than these?"

"Yes, Lord," he said, "you know that I love you."

Jesus said, "Feed my lambs."

Again Jesus said, "Simon son of John, do you love me?"

He answered, "Yes, Lord, you know that I love you."

Jesus said, "Take care of my sheep."

The third time he said to him, "Simon son of John, do you love me?"

Peter was hurt because Jesus asked him the third time, "Do you love me?" He said, "Lord, you know all things; you know that I love you."

Jesus said, "Feed my sheep." (vv. 15–17)

When they finished eating, Jesus broke the silence and asked Peter three consecutive times whether he loved him. The text says that by the third time Peter felt hurt by Jesus repeatedly asking him the same question. But on the night of Jesus's arrest, how many times had Peter been asked whether he knew Jesus? Three. How many times did Peter deny Jesus? Three. So could it be that Jesus, full of grace and mercy, wasn't trying to hurt Peter with his three questions but trying to heal him? It leads us to ask ourselves: Who do we have in our lives asking us the tough questions—not questions that hurt us but questions that heal?

There are all types of fires in the Bible, but there were only two that were distinctly called charcoal fires. One was the fire around which Peter denied Jesus. The other fire was the fire that Jesus made on the shore that morning, where Jesus redeemed Peter. Jesus reset the scene of Peter's denial, and it is in this place that he restored him. What could have been a reminder of Peter's greatest failure was reclaimed by the grace of God, and, from then on, every time Peter would stand around a fire, it would have triggered not the shame of his past but rather the activation of God's grace in his life. If we are willing to meet Jesus in the places we are wounded the deepest, we can see God perform his greatest miracles. If we are willing to go back to the scene of the wound, the mistake, the failure, the sin, and allow Jesus to reclaim that space, he can turn our mess into our miracle.

Note that Jesus never mentioned Peter's denial of him. He never even brought it up. This silence is significant, reflecting the essence of Jesus's approach to our failures and shortcomings. Instead of focusing on our past mistakes, Jesus directs his attention toward our potential. His actions and teachings embody a spirit of forgiveness and renewal. He doesn't point in condemnation to our pasts; he points with compassion to our futures. For he came into the world not to condemn it but to save it (John 3:17). This foundational principle is a cornerstone of the Christian faith. Jesus doesn't cancel; he restores. He sees beyond our failures, envisioning what we can become with his guidance and grace.

Maybe you need to meet with Jesus around that wound again today, around that weakness again. It's common to carry scars from our past, feeling like they define us. But Jesus invites us to bring these wounds to him, allowing his healing power to transform them. Perhaps that space can be reclaimed by the glory of God. Consider the possibilities if you allow grace to reset the scene in your life. What was once the place where you were most ashamed can now become the place where God performs his greatest miracles in your life. This transformative process is at the heart of spiritual growth and redemption. It's about turning our lowest points into testimonies of divine intervention and love.

Just like Peter's, your story can continue. In Acts 2:1–4, Peter was in an upper room praying with about 120 people. The Bible describes this momentous event saying that there came a sound like a rushing mighty wind, filling the house where they were sitting. This powerful and supernatural occurrence was a prelude to an even more astonishing sight: What looked like cloven tongues of fire appeared and sat upon each of them. They all began to speak in other languages, as the Spirit of God gave them utterance. This miraculous event marked the birth of the church and demonstrated the power and presence of the Holy Spirit. It signified a new beginning, not only for Peter, but for all who witnessed and participated in this divine phenomenon.

When they started speaking in this heavenly unknown language, they spilled out into the streets, looking crazy. The sight of these individuals speaking in tongues drew immediate attention and confusion from onlookers. People were saying things like, "Bro, look at these people. It's like they're drunk. It's like they've been sipping on a little somethin'. What did they have in that upper room? An open bar?" The astonishment and skepticism were palpable among the crowd. Then the Bible tells us that Peter stood up and said, "These people are not drunk, as you suppose. It's only nine in the morning!" (Acts 2:15). He told them that what they were witnessing was an act of God. Peter's bold proclamation served as a powerful counter to the disbelief and mockery, asserting the divine nature of the events unfolding before their eyes. He went on to preach the message upon which the New Testament church was built, delivering a sermon that cut to the hearts of his listeners and led to the conversion of thousands. This was the detonation of a joy bomb that rippled through history, one rooted in Peter's embrace of God's forgiveness.

Here we see the culmination of God's grace in the life of Peter. The transformation is so compelling. The man who was scared to confess his association with Jesus in front of a few strangers was now standing up in front of potentially thousands of people from all over the known world, declaring the gospel of Jesus Christ. This moment highlights the incredible journey of redemption and empowerment that Peter underwent. The place of Peter's greatest weakness became the place where God revealed his own glory. This story is a powerful reminder that we don't have to hide our broken pieces. It is with the broken pieces of our lives that God constructs his biggest platforms from which he displays his glory.

You have permission to say the quiet part out loud. How many people are trapped thinking they will never overcome a difficulty, setback, or sin in their lives who could be liberated by our shouting a testimony we're tempted to whisper? Scripture says that we, as a collective people, are overcome by the blood of the Lamb and the word of our testimony. Others won't know what God is capable of until we have the courage to declare what he has empowered us to conquer.

Embracing your imperfections and allowing God to work through them can lead to profound changes and the realization of your true purpose. God is not done with you. Regardless of what you've walked through, how many mistakes you've made, or who has counted you out, you are not canceled. Receive God's mercy, giving it to yourself and to others in even greater measure.

HAPPY ARE THE PASSIONATELY PURE

Blessed are the pure in heart,

for they will see God.

MATTHEW 5:8

I discovered my love for music at a young age. My family has eclectic tastes—my dad especially. In our "before Christ" years, we listened to everything from James Brown to AC/DC, from Onyx to Eric Clapton, from George Clinton to David Sanborn. Then Dad got saved, and our playlist shifted to Gary Oliver, Bryan Duncan, Kirk Franklin, and Fred Hammond. It was only a matter of time until we would discover child prodigy musician, singer, and songwriter Jonny Lang. My dad and I loved his music, starting with his first project, *Lie to Me*. If you had told me as a kid that I'd one day sit across the table from Jonny, I wouldn't have believed you, but it happened!

Around 2008 my band took a trip to Nashville, Tennessee, and we happened to get connected to Jonny through a mutual friend after one of his shows. Imagine having the opportunity to have a "breakfast dinner" with someone you've admired for years. He'd been through hard times and had recently started following Jesus. The chance to sit down with him and eat scrambled eggs and bacon at midnight felt surreal! The conversation we had that night left a lasting impression on me.

During our talk, Jonny shared about his recent conversion to Christianity and how God had rescued and transformed his life. He spoke about the future of influential musicians, singers, and songwriters in culture. He didn't believe that the most talented, most popular, or hardest-working people would necessarily rise to prominence. Instead, he believed that God was looking for people whose hearts, characters, ambitions, and intentions were pure—ones he could trust to elevate in the next season. Walking away from that encounter, I found myself asking God to give me that kind of heart and character. I knew I might never be the most talented, hardest working, or most liked. But I prayed to be someone who desires what God desires: "Take delight in the LORD, and he will give you the desires of your heart" (Psalm 37:4).

The principle here is straightforward but profound: God cares not only about what we achieve but how we achieve it. While our world often celebrates outward success and ambition, God values the purity of our hearts, the integrity of our characters, and the sincerity behind our ambitions and intentions.

It's important to make a distinction here between purity and perfection. Perfection is the absence of flaws, a standard no one can fully achieve, and an ideal that often leads to discouragement because it's impossible to meet. Purity, on the other hand, is about the state of our intentions and motives, even in the midst of our imperfections. God doesn't demand perfection, but he does call us to a pure heart that seeks to do his will above all else. A pure heart doesn't mean a flawless one; it means one that, despite its imperfections, is committed to honesty, humility, and surrender to God's guidance. In other words, purity is not about being without error but about being sincere, truthful, and undivided in our devotion. When we live this way, we open ourselves to experience pure happiness—a joy bomb whose aftermath is a heart unclouded by hidden motives, fully aligned with God.

When we seek to live with purity in heart and character, when we examine our ambitions and intentions before God, we place ourselves in a position where he can use us powerfully. This kind of integrity shapes us and keeps us grounded, even if we don't always understand where God is leading us or how he might use us. In the end it's not just about what we achieve but about who we become along the way, not just doing good but being good while we do it. People with pure hearts, solid characters, and intentions that honor God can make an impact that resonates far beyond their own reach.

God cares most about the heart: what drives us, what moves us, and what we believe about God and ourselves. One of the great kings of the Old Testament, King Saul, was appointed by the prophet Samuel. Scripture says that God gave Saul a new heart, and he began to prophesy during a time when he was being marked for service to the Lord as the king of Israel. "As Saul turned to leave Samuel, God changed Saul's heart, and all these signs were fulfilled that day. When he and his servant arrived at Gibeah, a procession of prophets met him; the Spirit of God came powerfully upon him, and he joined in their prophesying" (1 Samuel 10:9–11). He would later be crowned king of Israel. It's a fascinating observation that God gave Saul another heart.

We know the unfortunate fate of Saul, however. His heart turned cold toward God. "I regret that I have made Saul king, because he has turned away from me and has not carried out my instructions" (15:11). Even the heart that God gave Saul was not enough to sustain him through his reign. Because Saul could not keep his heart pure, God had to call another king into leadership. Saul looked the part but lacked the heart. When making his choice to replace Saul, God did not look at outward appearances; he looked on the inside. He told Samuel, who was distressed that God was passing over seemingly ideal candidates, not to focus on their external attributes but to consider the internal: "The LORD said to Samuel, 'Do not consider his appearance or his height, for I have rejected him. The LORD does not look at the things people look at. People look at the outward appearance, but the LORD looks at the heart'" (16:7). God sought someone who already had a heart aligned with his, rather than someone who needed a new heart bestowed upon him. He found this in David, a man after his own heart. "After removing Saul, he made David their king. God testified concerning him: 'I have found David son of Jesse, a man after my own heart; he will do everything I want him to do'" (Acts 13:22).

That is what pure intentions lead us to do—everything God wants us to do, not just what we want to do. To have a pure heart we must allow the Spirit of God to lead our whole life into alignment through submission to God's ways. When we decide to follow Jesus, we are choosing to make what was true about David true about us. That the Lord would say of us, "He will do everything I want him to do."

Consider this question carefully: *Am I truly committed to selling out wholeheartedly to do everything God wants me to do, which means doing nothing he doesn't?* This isn't a question to pass by lightly, for it reaches into the depths of our desires and ambitions and the direction of our lives. It's a question that requires us to look within, where motives lie hidden, where intentions are formed, and where the true state of our hearts and characters is known.

Imagine what it means to live fully in God's purpose, holding nothing back, no ambitions twisted toward self-interest, no motives clouded by compromise. It is a life not of divided focus or selective obedience but of pure, undivided devotion. Such a life isn't built on grand gestures or external perfection. It's built on the everyday surrender of our wills to God's, a quiet faithfulness that steadily chooses him above all else.

Take a moment. Sit with this question. Let it move beyond words and stir the deep places of your spirit. Ask yourself: *If God looked at my heart right now, would he see someone willing to be led fully by him? Would he find in me a heart that desires to do only what he wills, and nothing else?* This is not about achieving flawlessness but about holding a pure resolve—a resolve that says, "Lord, let my life be wholly yours. Shape my ambitions, refine my intentions, purify my character, until I am someone you can trust to do everything you want me to do."

INFORMED OR IN LOVE?

The teaching of Jesus on that Eremos hillside reveals to us the truth of an idea I once heard that it is not the greatness of intellect but the purity of affection that allows us to see God. This idea cuts to the core of the issue like a sharpened knife. Isn't it true that human arrogance often convinces us that through our intellect and knowledge we can uncover the realities of God? This impulse to discover God through intellectual ascent didn't begin with AI or our easy access to a universe of information online; it started back in Genesis 11, with the story of the Tower of Babel.

The story of the Tower of Babel shows what happens when people use their ambition and intellect not to grow closer to God but to try to make themselves equal to him. This struggle started long before Babel—Adam and Eve's mistake in Eden was that they weren't content just being with God and instead wanted to be like him. The story also demonstrates that when we are driven by self-serving motives, our collective efforts can lead us astray. I don't believe God was troubled by humanity's effort to achieve something great together. The problem was that their hearts were focused on doing something great for themselves, to see their names elevated in all the earth. Their motivation for unity was not intimacy with God but notoriety among people. Genesis 11:4 states, "Then they said, 'Come, let us build ourselves a city, with a tower that reaches to the heavens, so that we may make a name for ourselves; otherwise we will be scattered over the face of the whole earth.'" Their intention was clear: They sought fame and self-glorification, not a partnership with God to cultivate the world.

This ancient story is still alive in today's world. Not just alive in the world—it's alive in me! And it seems my kids have inherited this attitude from me. I say that in jest because my son Navy said something so funny a few years back that reinforces this reality. My wife told me about a conversation they had before bed one night after he was disciplined for acting up. Lorna was explaining to him that he didn't have "listening ears," to which he responded, "I heard you, but I wanna be the boss!" She reminded him that Mommy and Daddy are the bosses (in that order, I guess), to which he replied, "But I wanna be the boss because I wanna do what I wanna do!" The truth is, we may outgrow that level of honesty, but we seldom outgrow the truth in that confession. I know I haven't. I'm constantly checking my own motives, praying that my pursuit of wisdom and under-standing is grounded in a relationship with God.

In this modern age, how many of our ventures, our pas-sions, even our dreams come from places in our hearts that aren't pure? Think about it—why do we chase success, rec-ognition, or the need to know more, sometimes even about God? Often it's not just about getting closer to him but about feeling significant or validated. Our culture tells us that fame or recognition is a measure of worth, so we crave the spotlight thinking it's a quick way to fulfillment.

And there's more to it than just fame. Sometimes it's the fear of being vulnerable. Real intimacy with God, or anyone else, requires us to be fully open, to reveal our innermost selves. That's a hard thing to do. It's easier to reach for public praise than to bare our souls in private. Our world applauds fame, visibility, and influence, and it can fool us into thinking that's where the meaning lies.

But here's the truth—this chase for recognition often leaves us emptier than when we started. Fame, applause, accolades—they're fleeting. They satisfy for a moment, but they don't touch the deeper, lasting needs of our souls. We may think that achieving enough, knowing enough, or proving ourselves will fill that void, but it never does. Lasting fulfillment doesn't come from superficial applause. It comes from meaningful relationships, from purpose, from a life that's rooted in something deeper.

Social media doesn't help either. It tempts us with instant approval—likes, shares, and comments—feeding the craving for external validation. We create carefully curated versions of ourselves online, idealized, filtered. But it's a false reality, one that pushes us further from authenticity and intimacy.

Even in our careers, in competitive environments, we strive for recognition to open doors, to gain a reputation. But in all of this we often mistake notoriety for fulfillment. The applause might make us feel successful in the short term, but it doesn't satisfy the deeper parts of who we are.

Spiritually, too, we may find ourselves looking for meaning in the wrong places. Without a foundation in God, we might reach for fame or influence, trying to fill a void that only he can satisfy. A relationship with God can become more about collecting knowledge than forming a connection, leading us to seek answers and achievements outside of him.

My heart's desire isn't to gather information about God but to know him personally, intimately. I don't just desire to be informed about God; I want to remain truly in love with him.

True understanding of God doesn't come from knowledge alone; it's born from a heart surrendered to him, a heart that yearns to be close to him. The story of the Tower of Babel reminds us that our greatest accomplishments and the heights of our knowledge mean nothing if they aren't rooted in a genuine, humble relationship with our Creator. We have to turn our focus from glorifying ourselves to something more real—knowing God deeply, seeing as he sees.

This struggle isn't unique to us. Throughout Scripture we see people wrestling with the temptation to replace intimacy with knowledge, reducing a relationship with God to a list of rules or a stack of facts. Hosea 6:6 says, "I desire mercy, not sacrifice, and acknowledgment of God rather than burnt offerings." God's desire has always been for a sincere relationship, not just religious performance. Just as the people of Israel fell into the trap of empty ritual, we, too, can get caught in the habit of learning about God without getting to know him. The Scriptures warn of people who are "always learning but never able to come to a knowledge of the truth" (2 Timothy 3:7).

And it's so easy to be puffed up by knowledge. But as Paul reminded us, "Knowledge puffs up while love builds up" (1 Corinthians 8:1). Knowledge alone doesn't connect us to God; intimacy does. Knowing about him should lead us to know him more closely, to love him more fully.

As I read Peter Scazzero's *The Emotionally Healthy Leader*, one point struck me: Having access to information about someone isn't the same as having intimacy with them. God might know everything about us, but that doesn't mean we're inviting him into every part of who we are. David captured this beautifully in Psalm 139, where he reflected on how deeply God knows him. "Lord, you have all the information about me! There is nothing you don't know!" And yet he invited God into his heart: "Search me, God" (v. 23). It's a powerful moment—David wasn't just acknowledging that God has all the details; he was asking God to know him.

The Enemy would love for us to settle for a knowledge-based relationship with God, a relationship that might feel safe but lacks real connection. Remember Adam and Eve? After they sinned, they hid, thinking that putting distance between themselves and God would protect them. But God didn't ask, "What did you do?" He asked, "Where are you?" (Genesis 3:9). His desire was for them to invite him into their failure, their brokenness. Because of Jesus, we no longer have to hide from God; instead, we get to hide in him. As Paul said in Romans 8:1, "There is now no condemnation for those who are in Christ Jesus."

There's a great joy in letting go of impure motives. When we stop trying to work an angle with God or others, we find a kind of freedom. God isn't fooled by the things we say or do to get what we want. He sees our hearts, and he's not impressed by showmanship. Jeremiah 17:10 says, "I the LORD search the heart and examine the mind, to reward each person according to their conduct, according to what their deeds deserve." God wants a heart that's real, a heart that isn't afraid to be honest and vulnerable before him.

This isn't about grand gestures. It's about the quiet,

everyday moments when we choose him above all else. "Lord, search me. See my motives, test my heart, and lead me along the path of everlasting life." Imagine God saying of us, "They will do everything I want them to do." Let that be our aim— not perfection, but a pure, undivided devotion that's willing to trust, follow, and love God with all we have.

I don't think I've reached that place yet, and I know it's only by the grace of God that he has given me the platform I have. But I never want to lose sight of the joy bomb Jonny shared that night in that Nashville café: God is looking for hearts rather than talents to elevate; he wants not just the most accomplished people in any given field but those with hearts that can be trusted with the responsibility of pointing others to Jesus in every aspect of their lives.

LOVE, TO SEE IT

Isn't it interesting that Jesus connects a pure heart for God to a clear vision of him? "Blessed are the pure in heart, for they will see God." The formulation leads us to believe that loving God with a pure heart is more than an act of obedience; it's the very heartbeat of faith. It's what brings us to life, giving us eyes to see him. And this isn't some lofty idea reserved for saints in stained-glass windows—it's for all of us, right here and now. Hebrews 12:14 lays it out with clarity: "Pursue peace with all people, and holiness, without which no one will see the Lord" (NKJV). This isn't a suggestion or a box to check off on a list. It's a passionate pursuit, a life-shaping journey that unlocks a vision of God, bringing us into a place of wonder. It's the code to arming a joy bomb that when detonated gives way to clarity and happiness we'd never otherwise find.

Holiness isn't a set of rules or an antiquated moral code; it's a state of being that makes room for God's presence to flood our lives. It's the path to intimacy with God, the way our hearts clear the clutter, preparing us for something so profound that words can barely capture it. Holiness is where God meets us and reveals himself to us in ways that go beyond our expectations or understanding. And through holiness we unleash a joy bomb—a rush of God's joy, an explosion of divine delight that fills every corner of our souls. This is the joy that transforms us, sustains us, and affects everyone we encounter.

In a house with four boys and two dogs, things can get messy. Messes are a part of it, but sometimes I don't understand how spilled chocolate milk got into my sock drawer. If you're wondering, no one else knows either. One thing about boys is that they have to touch every single square inch of every single thing in their environment. So there are fingerprints everywhere. I was sitting in the living room recently, peering out the sliding glass doors that lead into our backyard. There are beautiful trees and plants. Our pups, Ranger and Ritzy, were roaming through the backyard. It's simple but picturesque. And then I started to see smudges, fingerprints, dried up chip residue, and what looked to be a face-print with dried saliva printed on the glass. The more I saw, the more I noticed. Pretty soon I had forgotten about the serene moment

I was just in. I could no longer see the sunlight beyond the slobber.

Sometimes life is like that. One minute you're beholding the beauty of God's goodness and then you begin to notice the streaks of bitterness, smudges of past hurts, fingerprints of self-righteousness, and thick smears of religiosity that distort the scene. Each stain blurs and blocks the light, making it hard to see the beauty just beyond.

Holiness is the act of wiping that glass clean. It's the intentional work of clearing away bitterness, surrendering hurts, and wiping away the mess self-made righteousness leaves behind. As each layer is removed, the view becomes clearer, and the fullness of God's beauty breaks through in vibrant color and breathtaking clarity. In the same way, holiness clears away the spiritual clutter that obscures our connection with God, allowing his presence and joy to flood into us. And once we see God in his fullness, that joy becomes transformative, filling every corner of our being and shining through us to touch everyone we encounter.

Think about that for a second. To "see God" isn't a small promise. It's not just about knowing facts about God or having good theology. It's about an encounter, a revelation, a face-to-face experience with the living God. When our hearts are pure—undivided, focused on him, free from distractions— suddenly we begin to see God's fingerprints in our lives in ways we'd miss otherwise. Holiness, then, is not a requirement in the way we think of rules; it's an invitation to get closer, to see and know God as we could never know him otherwise.

Someone once explained to me that to be holy is to be set apart for God and to be marked by a close relationship with him. Holiness is about belonging to God in every fiber of our being. It's not about striving to be morally superior or better than others; it's about setting our lives apart for something bigger than ourselves. It's about being so captured by love for God that everything else pales in comparison. Holiness isn't something we accomplish; it's something God accomplishes in us when we surrender ourselves to him completely. And here's the thing: The more we belong to God, the more clearly we see him.

Think of it this way. When you fall in love with someone, you're not checking off boxes or measuring your actions. You're captivated. You naturally start making decisions that nurture that relationship. That's what loving God and pursuing holiness is like. Holiness isn't a performance; it's an over-flow. It's the natural result of being so captivated by God's goodness, so in awe of his love, that you're willing to let go of anything that doesn't bring you closer to him. When we love God like that, holiness becomes the path we choose, not out of duty, but out of delight.

And this is where the joy bomb goes off. Holiness isn't about depriving ourselves of happiness; it's about setting the stage for a deeper, more profound joy. Psalm 16:11 tells us, "In Your presence is fullness of joy; at Your right hand are pleasures forevermore" (NKJV). This is a joy that the world can't give and the world can't take away. When we walk in holiness, we're walking into God's presence, and with his presence comes a joy that is explosive, transformative, and enduring.

A. W. Tozer is often reported to have said, "The pursuit of God requires a commitment to purity that is not content with half-measures." He's absolutely right. Loving God calls us to dive in fully, no holding back. It's a call to surrender everything, to let God purify our hearts and minds, to let him clear away the debris and distractions that keep us from seeing him. And when we do, when we open ourselves to this process, we find that God doesn't leave us empty—he fills us to overflowing with his joy, his peace, his presence. It's not about what we lose; it's about what we gain.

Purity sets the table for joy.

Think about it like clearing out a room. When you get rid of all the clutter, there's space to fill it with what matters. Holiness clears out the spiritual clutter so that God's joy can flow in like a river. And this joy isn't a fleeting emotion; it's an abiding joy that holds us steady, that grounds us. Jesus spoke about this kind of joy in John 15:10–11: "If you keep my commands, you will remain in my love. . . . I have told you this so that my joy may be in you and that your joy may be complete." Look at those connections he made—obedience, love, joy, and completeness.

THE BEAUTY OF WHOLE-INESS

When we align ourselves with God's heart and live in holiness, we experience a joy that is, as Jesus described, "complete"—a joy that is whole, perfect, and unbreakable. This isn't just a feeling; it's a state of being that goes beyond temporary happiness or fleeting satisfaction. It's something deeper and richer because holiness and wholeness are two sides of the same coin. There's a powerful relationship between the two: Where there is holiness, there is wholeness. A life that is whole is one that is holy, and a holy life is a whole one.

Let's dig into this: Holiness and wholeness both mean a state of being undivided, untainted, and set apart for something greater. In God, there is no fracture, inconsistency, or division. He is complete, the very definition of wholeness. And because he is holy, everything he touches, every place he dwells becomes whole. In other words, holiness is God's nature, his essence—and when we pursue holiness, we're moving toward completeness.

When our lives are broken by sin, doubt, or insecurity, we often try to fill those gaps with whatever feels good at the moment—success, approval, comfort. But it's like trying to patch a shattered vase with glue. We might look whole for a moment, but as soon as life shakes us up again, those cracks start to show. Holiness, however, is the glue that not only patches the broken places but brings our lives back to an unbreakable wholeness. God doesn't want to just fill in the gaps; he wants to make us whole from the inside out.

This is why Jesus talks about giving us a joy that is complete. He isn't just promising a dose of happiness; he's offering something transformational. To be whole in God means to live in a place of internal unity and integrity—a place where our thoughts, desires, actions, and spirits all line up with God's heart. When we pursue holiness, we're not just trying to be "good" or morally upright; we're stepping into alignment with God's completeness. The closer we come to him, the more we find that our fractured places are healed, our divided hearts are united, and our restless souls find peace. Holiness brings us into harmony with God, and in that harmony we experience a joy that is complete and unbreakable.

This wholeness changes how we approach life. When we're whole, we're no longer chasing things that can't fulfill us. We're not running after fleeting happiness, because we're anchored in something eternal. We're not searching for approval or validation, because we know we're already loved, already chosen, already complete in him. Holiness sets us apart from the relentless striving of the world and brings us into a place of rest and security. We live out of a place of fullness instead of a place of lacking. We're no longer trying to fill a void; we're living from the overflow of God's presence.

The relationship between holiness and wholeness is also beautifully illustrated in the New Testament with the word *shalom*. Often translated as "peace," shalom means far more than the absence of conflict. It's a term that encompasses wholeness, harmony, and completeness. To live in shalom is to live in a state of holistic peace—a state of being where every part of us is aligned with God's goodness, without division or conflict. When we pursue holiness, we're really pursuing shalom—a state of wholeness that radiates peace, joy, and fulfillment.

So holiness isn't about restriction; it's about restoration. It's about God taking the fragmented parts of our lives and making them whole. When we choose holiness, we're allowing God to make us into a place where his joy can dwell completely. We become living testimonies of his love, reflecting his wholeness to a world that is desperate for it.

This may seem counterintuitive to the illustration, but go here with me for a moment: Making a bomb—especially a powerful one like a nuclear bomb—is all about getting the details exactly right. First, the materials have to be super pure. If there's any junk mixed in, the reaction won't work as planned, and things could even go sideways. Holiness and integrity are a lot like that. It's about clearing out the clutter in our lives—the doubts, selfish motives, or anything that doesn't line up with God's heart—so we're more focused and ready to connect with him.

Then there's the precision. With a bomb, every part has to be placed just so, and everything needs to work together perfectly; even the smallest mistake can disarm it. Living with integrity is similar—it's about being consistent, keeping our actions, thoughts, and intentions lined up with what we believe. Holiness is like this constant, careful work to stay true and focused, letting God move in every area of our lives.

And then there's the big picture: the power that comes from it. When a bomb goes off, it releases an insane amount of energy that instantly changes everything around it. Holiness does something similar, but instead of causing destruction, it unleashes joy and strength. Once we're aligned with God and living with that focus and purity, it's as though a joy bomb goes off inside us. God's love and joy just start flowing out, transforming us and having an impact on everyone we meet. So, yeah, holiness isn't just about following rules—it's about clearing the way for something powerful and lasting to happen in us and through us.

Holiness is a pure component within the joy bomb. In God, through holiness, we are made whole. We're invited to rest in his completeness, to find joy in his presence, to let go of the endless striving for happiness and live in the fullness of his joy. This joy bomb is the gift of living in wholeness—a life in which every part of us is united in purpose, anchored in love, and filled with peace.

Pastor and theologian John Piper famously said, "God is most glorified in us when we are most satisfied in Him."[1] There's a deep truth here. Holiness leads us into satisfaction, into a joy that's based not on circumstances but on the rock-solid foundation of God's presence. When we're filled with God's joy, the pressures and stresses of life lose their power. We're no longer living for approval or achievement; we're living from a place of divine satisfaction, where God himself is our joy and our strength.

When God's joy bomb goes off in our lives, it changes everything. This is a joy that spills over, a joy that transforms us from the inside out, and it's contagious. People around us can sense it, even if they can't quite put their finger on it. There's a peace, a lightness, a sense of fulfillment that radiates from someone who is walking in the joy of the Lord.

This is the power of holiness — it has an impact on everyone around us.

When God's joy fills our lives, it changes us in ways that people around us can't help but notice. It's not just about feeling good. It's a peace and confidence that transforms how we interact with others, how we handle stress, and how we approach life. And here's the key: This joy is contagious. People sense it, even if they can't pinpoint exactly why you seem different.

Think about a stressful work environment. Most people are tense, hurried, and easily irritated. But when you carry God's joy, you bring a calming presence that influences the whole room. You're not just another person stressed by circumstances; you're grounded, unshaken. Others notice, and it often makes them curious. This calmness and confidence open doors for conversations about where your peace comes from.

God's joy also changes our relationships. When we're filled with his joy, we become more patient, kind, and forgiving. We're less likely to take offense, because we're secure in God's love and approval. This helps us handle conflicts better and creates a stronger foundation in our friendships and families. Imagine the impact on your marriage, friendships, or parenting when you're operating from a place of joy and wholeness instead of insecurity or frustration.

Living in God's joy also gives us freedom from the need for constant validation. We stop seeking approval from others because we know we're fully accepted by God. This makes us more genuine and approachable, which naturally draws people to us. They see an authenticity that's rare, and it often inspires them to look for the source of that joy themselves.

When a community, such as a church or small group, is filled with God's joy, it creates a warm, welcoming environment. People feel loved and safe to be themselves, which draws others in. It's the kind of place people want to be, because they can feel the peace and love that flow from people who are living in God's joy.

So when we're filled with God's joy, it's not just for us—it spills over, affecting everyone we encounter. Our calm, our kindness, our authenticity, and our peace become powerful witnesses to God's love in action, and that's something people can't ignore.

But let's keep it real. Holiness isn't easy. It requires us to let go of things that hold us back, to surrender parts of ourselves we'd rather keep hidden. Holiness isn't about perfection; it's about surrender. It's a daily choice to say, "God, I'm all in. I'm willing to let go of whatever is keeping me from you." And every time we surrender something to God, he fills that space with more of himself. This is where the joy bomb comes in. As we make room for God, he meets us with a joy that is richer, fuller, and longer lasting than anything the world can offer.

David knew this truth well. In Psalm 27:4, he wrote, "One thing I ask from the LORD, this only do I seek: that I may dwell in the house of the LORD all the days of my life, to gaze on the beauty of the LORD and to seek him in his temple." David's heart was set on one thing: seeing God. And this kind of vision comes only from a life that's surrendered, a life that's pure, a life that's holy. David wanted more than just knowledge about God; he wanted an encounter with him. Holiness is what clears the way for that kind of encounter, for that face-to-face experience with God's beauty and majesty. And that encounter? It releases a joy that's beyond words.

When we live in holiness, we're living in a way that positions us to see God in every part of our lives. We start noticing his hand in the small things, sensing his presence in the quiet moments, feeling his love in the places we'd least expect it. Holiness opens our spiritual eyes, and with that vision comes a joy that's anchored in something real and unshakable.

So what does this mean for us, right here and now? It means loving God with everything we have. It means surrendering ourselves to him, allowing him to purify our hearts and transform our desires. It's about living in holiness, not as a rule, but as a response to the love we have for him. And as we do this, God meets us with a joy that fills us to the brim, a joy that overflows, a joy that can't be contained.

This is the joy bomb—the joy that comes from knowing God, from seeing him clearly, from experiencing his presence in a way that transforms everything. It's the joy that Jesus promised us, the joy that is "complete," a joy rooted in his love and presence. When we pursue holiness, we're not giving up anything worthwhile; we're making room for the very thing our souls were made for. We're creating space for God to fill us with a joy beyond comprehension, a joy that holds us, grounds us, and overflows to bless others.

Holiness isn't a burden; it's a blessing. It's the path to experiencing the fullness of God's joy—an explosion of divine delight that touches every part of who we are. So let's lean in, let's go deeper, and let's make room for God to fill us with his joy, his peace, and his presence. Because in his presence there is fullness of joy, and nothing else compares.

HAPPY ARE THE RELENTLESSLY PEACEFUL

Blessed are the peacemakers, for they will be called children of God.

MATTHEW 5:9

PEACEMAKERS AND PEACE FAKERS

I share a house with my beautiful wife, Lorna, and four little dudes who are twelve, nine, seven, and four. As I'm attempting to get my thoughts out for this chapter, I have my AirPods in my ears and my AirPods Max on over them. Any parents with young kids can understand the reason for this without an explanation. But for all of you who may think this is a bit over the top and ridiculous, it is the only way I can get any semblance of peace and quiet to focus on this task of writing. The number of times a child says "Mom" or "Dad" in a day is incalculable—Lorna has even told them to call her "Zelda" at times just to hear a different word. Of course, this backfired when we were with some friends and they asked our youngest, Banner, "What's your mommy's name?" To which he replied— you guessed it—"Zelda." They were very, very confused!

The irony in this, of course, is that one of our sons blurted out from the back seat a few years ago, "Can I get some peace and quiet, please?!" We'd been exposed to his screams, bangs, crashes, and long indiscernible rants for years, and now *he* demanded peace and quiet! I don't blame him, though; peace is a hard thing to come by these days. Perhaps you don't have four boys with raised voices in the back seat, but there are other voices that shout at you, continually disturbing your peace. These are not just sonic intruders that steal our peace; they are intruders of the soul and mind. These modern intruders come in various forms. There's the incessant pinging of notifications from our phones, the endless stream of emails, the perpetual demands of work, and the constant barrage of news—often bad—that fills our screens. Social media, while connecting us in many ways, also serves as a source of comparison and judgment, eroding our sense of peace. Then there are the internal voices—our own thoughts, doubts, and fears—that can be just as loud and disruptive as any external noise.

There are many facets to peace and places where we need peace in our lives. There is an intrinsic relational peace, which Jesus was speaking to in his statement "Blessed are the peacemakers." That is peace between you and others, but to make peace one must first possess the ingredients of peace. We can't make peace with another person if we don't first have peace ourselves. Maybe your inner five-year-old is yelling from the back seat of your mind, *Can I have some peace and quiet, please?!* I know that has been the case for me. But this question assumes that there is someone who can hand us peace. It assumes that our lack of peace is someone else's problem to solve. There is faith and hope in that question, as well, because it suggests that there is a peace that can be possessed. Both assumptions are true, just not in the way we typically think. We carry some of the same ideas about peace as we do about joy, in that they are intangible concepts delivered to us by tangible possessions, people, or experiences. Unfortunately, the endless acquisition of those things typically gives us less peace, not more.

What is true, though, is that we do have someone who can give us peace; it just doesn't come through the person you may initially expect it to come from, and it doesn't come premade. God gives us the ingredients of peace. But *we* must make it. It's like receiving a recipe and all the necessary ingredients from a master chef, but we still need to do the work of combining them and cooking the dish. Paul encouraged the Philippian church about the possibility of peace. If anyone knew how to make peace, it was Paul. Like a good cook, he knew the ingredients needed to whip up a platter of peace, and he even knew how to cook peace in prison. Paul turned a prison into a kitchen!

The apostle Paul wrote the letter to the Philippians while he was imprisoned, likely in Rome around AD 61–62. Despite his circumstances, Paul's letter is filled with joy and encouragement. The church at Philippi was one of the earliest Christian communities in Europe, founded by Paul during his second missionary journey. The Philippians had a special place in Paul's heart, and his letter reflects his deep affection and gratitude for their support. Paul's situation was dire; he was facing the possibility of execution. Yet he used this time to encourage the believers in Philippi to remain steadfast in their faith. He began his letter by expressing his thankfulness for their partnership in the gospel and praying that their love would abound more and more in knowledge and depth of insight. Even while imprisoned, Paul maintained a positive outlook and encouraged the Philippians to rejoice in the Lord always.

In Philippians 4:6–7, Paul wrote, "Do not be anxious about anything, but in every situation, by prayer and petition, with thanksgiving, present your requests to God. And the peace of God, which transcends all understanding, will guard your hearts and your minds in Christ Jesus." This passage provides a practical approach to achieving peace. Paul emphasized the importance of prayer and thanksgiving as antidotes to anxiety. He assured the Philippians that God's peace, which surpasses all human understanding, would protect their hearts and minds.

Paul went on to provide further instructions in Philippians 4:8–9: "Finally, brothers and sisters, whatever is true, whatever is noble, whatever is right, whatever is pure, whatever is lovely, whatever is admirable—if anything is excellent or praiseworthy— think about such things. Whatever you have learned or received or heard from me, or seen in me—put it into practice. And the God of peace will be with you." Here Paul highlighted the importance of focusing on positive and virtuous things. By directing their thoughts toward what is good and practicing what they had learned from Paul, the Philippians could experience the presence of the God of peace.

Paul's teachings in the book of Philippians are profound because they demonstrate that peace is not dependent on external circumstances but on one's relationship with God. His ability to find peace amid imprisonment is a testament to his deep faith and trust in God's sovereignty. Paul's letter encourages believers to seek peace through prayer, gratitude, and focused attention, regardless of whatever prison they find themselves in. This is a powerful reminder that peace is not the absence of trouble but the presence of God amid trouble. In today's world creating peace might involve setting boundaries with our technology, practicing mindfulness, cultivating gratitude, and seeking moments of stillness amid the chaos. It means intentionally choosing to focus on the good, the true, and the beautiful in our lives. It means trusting that even when life is noisy and chaotic, there is a deeper peace available to us.

So when your inner child yells for peace and quiet, remember that it is possible. It might take effort and intentionality, but the ingredients are there. We have the promise of peace from the ultimate source, and it's up to us to make it.

Like Jesus telling people how to be happy on the desolate hillside of Eremos, Paul was in an unexpected place to be inspired to write about peace—a Roman prison cell. Much of his writing was written from the center of God's will yet in the middle of trouble, struggle, and persecution. Isn't it interesting that Paul was actually in God's will when he encountered so many difficult circumstances?

It's common for modern Christians to use the absence of conflict as proof that they are walking in God's will. You'll often hear sincere followers of Jesus who are considering a major life decision use a feeling of peace as the sign of God's direction. Sometimes, of course, that's true. It's also true that if you always wait to feel peace before you obey God's call to pivot in life or make a difficult decision, you may delay your obedience. Peace is a poor gauge of God's will. Sometimes tension, pressure, and pain are better indicators that you're moving in the right direction. It's a common misconception that following God's will should always lead to a peaceful and smooth path. The Bible is filled with examples of faithful followers who faced immense challenges and hardships precisely because they were on the path God set for them. For instance, James 1:2–4 says, "Consider it pure joy, my brothers and sisters, whenever you face trials of many kinds, because you know that the testing of your faith produces perseverance. Let perseverance finish its work so that you may be mature and complete, not lacking anything."

Tension, pressure, and pain can serve as reminders that we are engaged in something significant and meaningful. When we encounter resistance, it often means we are stepping out of our comfort zones and into the areas where God is calling us to make an impact. Just as muscles grow stronger through resistance and stress, our spiritual growth is accelerated through trials and tribulations. These experiences force us to rely more on God and less on our own understanding and abilities. Romans 5:3–4 echoes this, stating, "Not only so, but we also glory in our sufferings, because we know that suffering produces perseverance; perseverance, character; and character, hope."

The peace that Paul promised in Philippians 4 is one that transcends our grasp on our reality and extends our faith toward a greater one. It is an unwavering assurance that no matter what we face, God is in control and his plans for us are good. Isaiah 26:3 promises, "You will keep in perfect peace those whose minds are steadfast, because they trust in you." By fostering a strong connection with God through daily spiritual practices—such as reading Scripture, praying, worshipping, and meditating on his promises—we can maintain this peace even during life's storms.

This God-given peace empowers us to navigate the challenges of life with confidence and hope, knowing that we are not alone and that our trials have a purpose. It transforms our perspective, enabling us to see beyond our immediate difficulties to the greater work God is doing in and through us. As Jesus reassures us in John 16:33, "I have told you these things, so that in me you may have peace. In this world you will have trouble. But take heart! I have overcome the world."

Colossians tells us to let peace rule in our hearts. Peace may not be the authority or the reality in every area of our external lives, but if we make peace and allow it to reign and rule in our hearts, becoming the governing authority of our interior world, we can face the same obstacles, heartbreaks, and losses Paul experienced and still allow the deep current of God's peace to steady us in any circumstance.

We have the ingredients for peace. First we pray, asking God for what we need with gratitude in our hearts. Then we guide our thoughts toward truth, honor, righteousness, purity, beauty, and other good things. These are not the ingredients the world, the culture, or even our own thoughts give us. The world gives us the ingredients to make fear, anxiety, and depression. Like Jesus, Paul points us to our thought life.

Please indulge me in another kitchen illustration. When my wife is cooking ooey-gooey chocolate chip cookies, there is an aroma that fills the kitchen, then the living room, and even drifts upstairs. The smell of goodness that fills the air is determined by what is baking in the oven. When you put the ingredients of goodness in the oven of your mind, you don't just make the product of peace; you create an atmosphere of peace in your life.

Creating an atmosphere of peace means that the peace within us becomes so strong and pervasive that it affects everything around us. Just as the aroma of baking cookies fills the entire house, the peace that God gives us can permeate every aspect of our lives. This atmosphere influences our interactions with others, our decisions, and our responses to challenges. It becomes a stabilizing force that others can sense and be drawn to.

An atmosphere of peace also means that our internal state is not easily disturbed by external circumstances. When we cultivate peace through our connection with God, we build a resilience that helps us remain calm and composed in the face of adversity. This inner peace acts like a thermostat, regulating the emotional climate of our lives, rather than allowing external events to dictate the temperature of our feelings.

Furthermore, this atmosphere can be a powerful testimony to others. People are often drawn to those who exhibit a calm and peaceful demeanor, especially in stressful situations. Our peace can serve as a witness to the transformative power of a relationship with God, showing that it is possible to have tranquility and assurance even in a turbulent world.

To create and maintain this atmosphere, we must continually focus on God and his promises. This involves praying regularly, meditating on Scripture, and aligning our thoughts with his truth. By filling our minds with positive and godly thoughts, we can sustain an environment of peace that blesses not only ourselves but also those around us.

Looking back at Jesus's words "Blessed are the peacemakers," I can admit that I've misread this scripture. I've read it as "Blessed are the peace*keepers*." Maybe you've done the same thing, believing that a person who avoids conflict is a person who lives in peace—but that's the furthest thing from what Jesus was communicating. Jesus was not averse to conflict. We will talk more about this shortly, but suffice it to say that he brought so much disturbance to the peace that he was executed. By not keeping the peace, going along to get along, or submitting to the pressure to not make a stir, he made peace possible.

PEACEKEEPERS OR PEACE TAKERS

Peacekeepers avoid getting into conflicts, having difficult conversations, and taking a stand for what's right.

To keep peace in this sense is not setting the groundwork for happiness for long because a conflict avoided is a conflict escalated. *Keeping* peace can feel like a cycle of hopelessness because to get along in a friendship, relationship, marriage, and so on your true feelings must be avoided. To *make* peace is courageous. To make peace you must be willing to share true thoughts, find places of compromise, and consider another's perspective.

"Blessed are the peace*makers*" might be misinterpreted as "Blessed are the peace*keepers*." But there's a fundamental difference between the two. The concept of being a peacemaker involves actively working toward reconciliation and justice, whereas being a peacekeeper often means maintaining the status quo to avoid conflict. This distinction is crucial in understanding Jesus's teachings and his mission on earth.

Peacekeepers often aim to avoid conflict, striving for harmony by maintaining the status quo. Their goal is to preserve peace even if it means compromising on truth or justice. This approach can lead to superficial harmony but fails to address the underlying issues that cause conflict. Peacekeepers may avoid difficult conversations and decisions, leading to unresolved tensions and injustices. Their focus is on maintaining outward appearances of peace, often at the expense of real, lasting solutions.

In contrast, peacemakers actively work to resolve conflicts, even if it means confronting uncomfortable truths. They strive to create true peace by addressing underlying issues and injustices. Peacemakers understand that genuine peace cannot be achieved without dealing with the root causes of conflict. They are willing to engage in difficult conversations and make tough decisions to bring about reconciliation and justice. This approach requires courage, patience, and a deep commitment to truth and fairness.

Examining the life of Jesus reveals that he did not shy away from conflict. On the contrary, he frequently engaged in it. His actions and teachings often created a clear distinction between his kingdom agenda and the prevailing religious and political agendas. Jesus's approach to peace was not about avoiding conflict but about addressing and resolving it to bring about reconciliation and justice.

Jesus was not afraid to ruffle feathers. He spoke truth to power, whether it was religious leaders or political authorities. His critiques of the Pharisees and Sadducees often led to heated confrontations. For example, in Matthew 23, Jesus delivered a series of harsh rebukes to the religious leaders, calling them hypocrites and blind guides. He criticized their legalism and their failure to understand the deeper principles of justice, mercy, and faithfulness. By challenging the religious authorities, Jesus exposed the hypocrisy and corruption that had become entrenched in the religious system.

Jesus sided with the unlikely and marginalized. His interactions with tax collectors, sinners, and Samaritans were controversial and challenged societal norms. By associating with those who were considered outcasts, Jesus demonstrated that God's love and grace were available to everyone, regardless of their social status or past actions. For example, in Luke 19, Jesus visited the house of Zacchaeus, a tax collector who was despised by his fellow Jews. This act of kindness and acceptance led to Zacchaeus's repentance and his commitment to making restitution for his wrongs.

Jesus's teachings were revolutionary and countercultural. He did not shy away from making statements that upset the established order. In the Sermon on the Mount, as we have seen, Jesus presented a radical vision of God's kingdom that challenged the prevailing values of his time. He taught that true righteousness goes beyond outward actions and encompasses the attitudes of the heart. He emphasized the importance of mercy, forgiveness, and love for one's enemies. These teachings were a stark contrast to the legalistic and retributive mindset of the religious leaders.

Jesus explicitly stated his purpose to bring not peace but a sword (Matthew 10:34). This statement highlights that his mission was not to maintain superficial harmony but to initiate profound transformation. Jesus's message often put him at odds with the established religious and social order. In Luke 12:51–53, Jesus stated that his coming would cause division even within families, as people would be divided over their responses to his message. This division was not an end but a means to clarify the choice that each person had to make regarding their allegiance to God's kingdom.

Jesus's refusal to conform or avoid conflict led to his execution, thereby creating the possibility for true peace through reconciliation with God. His death on the cross was the culmination of his mission to bring about reconciliation and justice. Through his sacrifice, Jesus broke down the barriers of sin and hostility, making it possible for all people to be reconciled to God and to one another.

Understanding Jesus as a peacemaker, rather than a peacekeeper, reshapes our view of his mission and teachings. He exemplified that true peace comes not from avoiding conflict but from confronting and resolving it, even at great personal cost. Jesus was a revolutionary who sought to bring about profound transformation in individuals and society. His teachings called for a radical reorientation of one's life and priorities, challenging the prevailing values and norms of his time.

Jesus's ministry was marked by a commitment to addressing injustices and bringing about reconciliation. He spoke out against the hypocrisy and corruption of the religious leaders and challenged societal norms that marginalized certain groups. By doing so, Jesus demonstrated that true peace cannot be achieved without addressing the underlying issues that cause conflict.

Living as peacemakers requires a commitment to truth. This means being honest about the issues that cause conflict and division, even when it is uncomfortable or unpopular. It involves a willingness to speak out against injustice and to advocate for what is right, even when it comes at a personal cost.

For example, in the realm of social justice, being a peacemaker may involve speaking out against systemic racism, advocating for the rights of marginalized groups, and challenging policies and practices that perpetuate inequality. It requires a willingness to confront uncomfortable truths about the ways in which our society falls short of the ideals of justice and equality.

Peacemakers must also be committed to the pursuit of justice. This means working to address the root causes of conflict and injustice, rather than simply trying to maintain superficial harmony. It involves advocating for systemic changes that promote fairness and equality, and working to create a society that reflects the values of God's kingdom.

In the context of economic inequality, being a peacemaker may involve advocating for policies that promote fair wages, affordable housing, and access to health care and education. It requires a commitment to addressing the underlying issues that contribute to poverty and inequality, and working to create a more just and equitable society.

Living as peacemakers also involves a commitment to reconciliation and healing. This means working to repair broken relationships and to bring about reconciliation between individuals and communities. It involves a willingness to forgive and to seek forgiveness, and to work toward healing the wounds that have been caused by conflict and division.

In personal relationships, being a peacemaker may involve seeking to repair a broken relationship with a family member or friend. It requires a willingness to confront the issues that caused the conflict, to seek forgiveness and to offer forgiveness, and to work toward rebuilding trust and understanding.

The church has a crucial role to play in promoting peace and justice in the world. As followers of Jesus, we are called to be peacemakers, working to bring about reconciliation and justice in our communities and in the world. This involves a commitment to truth, justice, and reconciliation, and a willingness to engage in the challenging work of addressing the underlying issues that cause conflict and division.

The church can play a crucial role in advocating for justice and working to address the root causes of conflict and injustice. This involves speaking out against injustice, advocating for policies that promote fairness and equality, and working to create a society that reflects the values of God's kingdom.

The church also has a role to play in educating its members about the issues that cause conflict and injustice, and in raising awareness about the importance of being peacemakers. This involves teaching about the principles of justice and reconciliation and providing opportunities for members to engage in advocacy and action.

In contrast to the peacemakers are the "peace takers." If you don't know any . . . you may be one. Sorry! A peace taker is easily offended, yet happy to offend; is quick to share an opinion and slow to listen to someone else's; is constantly embroiled in drama; is generally negative; and dwells on past hurts.

Peace takers are usually bosses, not leaders; gossips, not encouragers; and critics, not collaborators. The difference is like night and day. A boss is like a drill sergeant, barking orders and demanding obedience, which creates a vibe of fear and stress. Leaders, however, are like coaches, cheering everyone on and helping them reach their best, making the whole team feel pumped and ready to tackle any challenge.

Gossips are like mosquitoes, buzzing around and spreading negativity everywhere they go. They focus on other people's mistakes and flaws, making everyone feel on edge. Encouragers, on the other hand, are like sunshine after a storm, bringing warmth and positivity. They celebrate wins, give helpful advice, and lift everyone up, creating a feel-good atmosphere.

Peace takers are also like potholes in the road slowing everyone down, pointing out problems but not helping to fix anything. Critics are like heavy rain clouds, always ready to dump on the parade. Collaborators, though, are like gardeners, planting seeds of ideas and working with others to help them grow. They create an environment where everyone feels valued and excited to pitch in.

The big problem with being a peace taker is that you can't snatch peace from others and expect to feel joy yourself. True happiness comes from building and nurturing good vibes with others, not from tearing people down. When you take peace from others, it's like kicking over a sandcastle—you ruin their fun and end up feeling crummy too. This negative cycle just keeps everyone feeling down.

On the flip side, people who make peace spread joy like wildfire. Making peace takes effort, just as planting a garden does—it needs care, patience, and a bit of demanding work. But the results are worth it. Actions such as showing empathy, being kind, and forgiving create strong, healthy relationships. When you help build a positive and supportive environment, it's like creating a comfortable, cozy home where everyone, including you, can feel happy and safe.

Being a peace taker leaves you feeling isolated, like a lone wolf. But being a peacemaker connects you with others, making life richer and more fulfilling. By choosing to be a leader, encourager, and collaborator, you make life better for everyone around you and fill your own life with positive, meaningful experiences.

Those who make peace experience joy. Making anything takes work, commitment, and focus, but peace is always worth the effort because making peace pleases God. To make peace we use the materials of compassion, kindness, resolve, forgiveness, understanding, humility, Scripture, and the Spirit of God. We ought to fight for one another, not against. In this we are God's children.

Children don't hold on to grudges or harbor bitterness. Getting to the apology can sometimes be hard work, but moving on past the apology is often a breeze. God uses the picture of us as his children because we will never look more like him than when we are operating in an effort for peace. This is what Christ did for us. He made peace with the wrath of God, enduring our punishment and taking our sin so that we might be called the sons and daughters of God.

HAPPY ARE THE WILLINGLY PERSECUTED

Blessed are those who are persecuted

because of righteousness, for theirs

is the kingdom of heaven.

MATTHEW 5:10

HAPPINESS IN HARD PLACES

Happy are the persecuted. This is a challenging, difficult statement, and one to be handled with care. But the reality is that when we are alienated, shunned, and even made to suffer for following Jesus, we lay claim to the kingdom—and can experience joy. The same joy Jesus possessed when facing the persecution of the cross. "For the joy set before him he endured the cross, scorning its shame, and sat down at the right hand of the throne of God" (Hebrews 12:2).

This verse highlights the incredible endurance and perspective of Jesus. Despite the intense suffering and shame associated with crucifixion, Jesus was able to look beyond his immediate circumstances. The "joy set before him" refers to the ultimate victory and fulfillment of God's redemptive plan for humanity. Jesus knew that his suffering would lead to the salvation of countless souls, reconciliation between God and man, and the establishment of his eternal kingdom. This profound joy and purpose allowed him to endure the agony of the cross. This shows us that our joy must be "set," and set joy leads to strong commitment.

The phrase "scorning its shame" emphasizes Jesus's disregard for the disgrace that came with crucifixion. In ancient times crucifixion was considered one of the most humiliating and painful forms of execution. But Jesus chose to embrace this path, focusing not on the shame but on the glorious outcome—his exaltation and the salvation of believers. By sitting "at the right hand of the throne of God," Jesus is now in a position of honor and authority, having completed his earthly mission and triumphed over sin and death.

When persecution and suffering surround us, we must set joy before us, fixing our focus on the eternal reality of being in God's great presence forever. We endure our crosses, our pain, our pressing with purpose. Jesus wanted to make clear to his followers that hard times, difficulty, and danger would come, but, as a reward for our genuine faith and steadfast love, we would gain the ultimate treasure: heaven (Matthew 5:10–12).

There have been moments throughout my faith walk when I have struggled to make sense of the difficulties I've experienced personally or helplessly watched others face. I've been in worship services singing words to songs that declared truths that seemed to contradict what I or others in tough situations were experiencing. I've sung about how God is undefeated and never loses battles while feeling as though I was in the middle of a losing streak. I've heard myself proclaiming God's healing power while seemingly not seeing that power at work in the lives of those fighting physical battles every single day.

It seems at times what we proclaim to be true about God is held in uncomfortable tension with what we perceive to be happening in our lives and in the world. This tension can lead to doubts about God, his ability, and his involvement in the details of our lives. The truth is that it's impossible to reconcile these doubts when we have only one reality in view. We must step back from the temporary vantage point from which we view our lives. If we look at things only in isolation, in one dimension, all we are left with is pain, disappointment, and confusion.

I had the chance to watch a potter at work with a piece of clay on the potter's wheel once. It was amazing to watch her work. With each rotation the potter applied pressure—sometimes gentle, other times firm—to mold the clay into a beautiful and useful vessel. To the untrained eye the process might look harsh. The clay was pressed, stretched, and occasionally even collapsed, only to be reshaped again. But the potter never lost sight of the final design, even when the clay appeared to be a formless mess.

This is what our lives can feel like in seasons of pain and suffering—spinning, pressed, and seemingly falling apart under the weight of circumstances. Yet when we step back and trust the hands of the divine Potter, we realize every press, every stretch, and even every collapse is intentional. God is shaping us into something far greater than we could imagine, preparing us for a purpose beyond what we can currently see.

Before we step back to consider life from a broader perspective, we must first consider the light in which we see God. There is a beautiful duality to the nature of God. Two realities exist within him: his transcendence and his immanence (Isaiah 57:15; Jeremiah 23:23–24).

God is transcendent. He is beyond the material, beyond time and space, beyond logic and reason to an infinite degree. Because he is transcendent, sickness can't touch him, sin can't reach him, doubt can't debunk him, brokenness can't break him, fear can't fool him, and the devil can't dethrone him. He's the beyond-God! Yet he also carries this strand of immanence in his divine DNA. *Immanence* simply means closeness. He plainly displayed his immanence by taking on human flesh, by becoming the God-man—Immanuel, God with us. He became human to share an unparalleled closeness with humanity.

Through Jesus, he showed humanity that he was not a God beyond tears; he would weep himself. As John 11:35 poignantly states, "Jesus wept." This shortest verse in the Bible carries immense weight, showing that God in the flesh could feel and express human grief. He is not a God beyond heartache, for he would face betrayal and criticism as a man (Isaiah 53:3).

It's the Potter with infinite vision whose hands are gently shaping us. In every trial and pressing he is molding us into vessels that will carry his glory and reflect his joy—both now and into eternity.

He knew the pain of witnessing a loved one's death and the sorrow that soaks the soul. It's remarkable that God would have the power to call Lazarus out of the grave but also possess the compassion to wrap his arms around the women weeping over the brother they had buried. This duality is vividly depicted in John 11:33–35, where Jesus was deeply moved by the mourning of Mary and the others, and he wept with them before performing the miracle of raising Lazarus.

Consider the profound duality in the book of Mark, where Jesus encountered a woman who had suffered for years, who was beyond the help of physicians. Even though this woman only touched Jesus's clothes, she was healed. Mark 5:25–34 recounts this story, showing that Jesus was divine enough to know what to do to heal this woman's body, but he was also human enough to know the words to say to heal her soul. He called her "daughter." He told her, "Go in peace and be freed from your suffering." This simple yet profound interaction highlights his deep understanding of human suffering and his ability to heal both body and soul.

In his transcendence God exists outside of time and suffering, yet in his immanence he willingly stepped into it. Philippians 2:6–8 beautifully encapsulates this mystery: "Who, being in very nature God, did not consider equality with God something to be used to his own advantage; rather, he made himself nothing by taking the very nature of a servant, being made in human likeness. And being found in appearance as a man, he humbled himself by becoming obedient to death— even death on a cross!"

God's transcendence means he is the ultimate authority, unrivaled and unsurpassed. His immanence means he is the ultimate companion, empathetic and understanding. Together, these aspects of God reveal a being who is both majestic and intimate, both powerful and personal. This divine paradox is at the heart of the Christian faith, offering a God who is far beyond us yet closer than our very breath.

In the New Testament the incarnation of Jesus is the ultimate merger of God's transcendence and immanence. As stated in John 1:14, "The Word became flesh and made his dwelling among us. We have seen his glory, the glory of the one and only Son, who came from the Father, full of grace and truth." Jesus's ministry was marked by acts of compassion and miracles, demonstrating God's power and his personal care. He healed the sick, raised the dead, fed the hungry, and comforted the sorrowful.

Jesus's parables often revealed the nature of God's kingdom and his relational approach. In the parable of the prodigal son (Luke 15:11–32), Jesus illustrated God's readiness to forgive and restore those who return to him. The father's joyous embrace of his returning son exemplifies God's immanent love and mercy, welcoming us despite our failings.

In the Sermon on the Mount, Jesus addressed the worries of daily life, assuring his followers of God's intimate concern for their needs. Matthew 6:25–34 encapsulates this message, where Jesus told his disciples not to worry about their lives, what they would eat or drink, or about their bodies and what they would wear. He reminded them of God's provision for the birds of the air and the flowers of the field, emphasizing that the disciples were much more valuable to him.

Jesus's miracles also serve to demonstrate his immanent care for individuals. In Mark 7:31–37, Jesus healed a man who was deaf and nonspeaking. Instead of performing this miracle publicly, he took the man aside privately, touched his ears and tongue, and spoke a healing command. This personal approach shows Jesus's sensitivity to the man's condition and dignity.

The book of Hebrews further elucidates Jesus's role as our high priest, who bridges the gap between God and humanity. Hebrews 4:14–16 states,

> Therefore, since we have a great high priest who has ascended into heaven, Jesus the Son of God, let us hold firmly to the faith we profess. For we do not have a high priest who is unable to empathize with our weaknesses, but we have one who has been tempted in every way, just as we are—yet he did not sin. Let us then approach God's throne of grace with confidence, so that we may receive mercy and find grace to help us in our time of need.

This passage highlights Jesus's unique position as both divine and human, capable of understanding our struggles and interceding on our behalf. It invites believers to confidently seek God's mercy and grace, knowing that he understands and cares deeply for them.

The Revelation to John provides a glimpse of the transcendent and immanent God in the vision of the new heaven and new earth. Revelation 21:3–4 proclaims, "And I heard a loud voice from the throne saying, 'Look! God's dwelling place is now among the people, and he will dwell with them. They will be his people, and God himself will be with them and be their God. "He will wipe every tear from their eyes. There will be no more death" or mourning or crying or pain, for the old order of things has passed away.'" This vision of the future affirms the ultimate fulfillment of God's immanence, where he will be permanently present with his people, eradicating all forms of suffering.

From the Old Testament to the New Testament, from creation to the consummation of history, God reveals himself as the sovereign Lord of all and the intimate companion of humanity. This divine paradox enriches our understanding of God, offering a profound sense of his majesty and a comforting assurance of his nearness.

God's transcendence means he is the King of kings, the Lord of lords, the Alpha and the Omega, the beginning and the end. His immanence means he is the Shepherd who seeks the lost, the Father who welcomes the prodigal, the Friend who lays down his life. This multifaceted nature of God invites believers into a relationship that is deeply personal and eternally awe-inspiring.

How incomprehensible that the transcendent God who commands the cosmos is the same immanent God who whispers in our hearts. He is the sovereign King and the gentle Shepherd, the mighty warrior and the tender healer. In Jesus we see the full expression of this divine mystery, a God who is beyond all yet present in all, inviting us into a relationship that is as profound as it is personal. This is the God who reigns supreme yet walks alongside us, the God who is infinitely great yet intimately near, the God who is both our Creator and our Comforter.

MOMENTARY PAIN LEADS TO ETERNAL JOY

What we understand about the character of God matters so much because it informs and frames how we think about everything else. If we see Jesus as a powerful but faraway God, we may not believe he cares about us. On the other hand, if we see Jesus only as a kind, wise man, we may believe that he came merely to help us, not to save us. Seeing a God that exists within our reality and beyond it awakens us to the notion that there is a reality that we exist in and still one beyond it. Serious students of the Bible call these realities the temporal and the eternal. That just means that there's a now and there's a forever.

Many people today start with the now and use it to frame forever. Faith in Jesus gives us the ability to flip that perspective and start with what we know about forever to help us define and process what we're experiencing now. If we focus only on our devastating pain, loss, or failure, we'll believe that pain, loss, and failure will last forever. We will doom ourselves to callously believing that there is nothing more to hope for beyond the moments when the bottom fell out. But if there is an eternity in which endless joy, permanent peace, and overwhelming love flow from the goodness of the glory of God, we can maintain an abiding hope that anchors us when the tides of unexpected difficulties rise.

Amid persecution and imprisonment the apostle Paul wrote, "Our present sufferings are not worth comparing with the glory that will be revealed" (Romans 8:18). The ability to endure persecution is the greatest proof of God's favor, because God doesn't just show favor through the good he brings into our lives, but at times he shows his favor through the pain he allows.

Paul made this shift in perspective. He had what he referred to as a "thorn in my flesh" (2 Corinthians 12:7). Scholars have debated what he was referring to, and although we don't know the specifics, surely we can all relate to having something in our lives that causes us to ache, a wound that we live with, something that keeps us up at night and is the first thing on our minds in the morning. I know I've had mine. In Scripture we see Paul pray and plead with God to remove the thorn in his flesh, but God didn't do it. Then Paul made a statement that changed everything—for him and for us. Paul said, "I consider that our present sufferings are not worth comparing with the glory that will be revealed." What he was pointing us toward is the fact that there is a horizon called eternity, a reality beyond our experience that gives us hope. Even in our suffering we know that our suffering has an expiration date. Weeping may indeed endure for a night or what seems like thousands of nights, but there is a joy that comes in the morning with a sun that shines so bright that darkness ceases to exist.

It's my prayer that this ultimate reality frames your present reality. We know that if our faith has been securely placed in Jesus, there is a dawn coming that carries the hues of happiness emanating from the Son. We will step across the threshold of time and space into eternity and only experience the glory of God! That is our ultimate joy. As we have seen, the Scriptures tell us that in his presence is the fullness of joy. Every aspect of joy we feel here and now in its varying degrees will only be intensified by our proximity to God's presence in eternity. That's a truth we can build our hopes upon. It doesn't answer all our questions or satisfy all our doubts, but it does give us the promise of God's presence in the middle of them, and it gives way to a joy that will carry us to that great day.

JOY SHINING THROUGH THE PAIN

I couldn't believe it. I thought my wife and I had a pact, an unspoken vow of solidarity. I had assumed that there were some things exclusively between the two of us, secrets that no man, woman, or child could breach. Ever since the boys were little, I'd tell each of my sons, at separate times, that he was my favorite. I'd been doing this for years, having each one convinced that he was my favorite! None of them ever caught on to the possibility that I was telling them all the same thing. The only one who knew was my confidante and soulmate, Lorna.

That is, until that fateful evening sitting around the kitchen counter with our four boys. They were fresh out of the pool, the pizza was hot, the cola was flowing, and the laughs were on tap. It was one of those perfect family moments that you wish you could bottle up and keep forever. The kids were happy, the atmosphere was light, and everything seemed right. My oldest son, Kanaan, piped up with a grin on his face, "Dad just told me earlier that I was his favorite son!" His statement was filled with pride, and he looked around expecting the usual playful banter from his brothers.

Then my second-oldest son, Lawson, not wanting to be outdone, said, "No, Dad's been telling me that I'm his favorite for years!" He said it with a mixture of confidence and defiance, clearly proud of his special status. This was followed up by my third son, who exclaimed, "What?!" with a look of pure shock and disbelief on his face.

Uh-oh. Things got complicated in a hurry! I was ready to quickly clean this up with the help of Lorna. She started to speak before I could form a sentence and bluntly stated, "Hate to break it to you boys, but your dad tells all of you the same thing!" The room fell silent. You could hear a pin drop. The boys stared at her, then at me, processing what they had just heard.

How could she? I was betrayed and bewildered! The illusion had been shattered. My response to the truth bomb was a witty reply, trying to salvage the situation. "My favorite son knows who he is!" I said with a wink, attempting to keep the belief alive. The boys looked at one another, then back at me, trying to decide whether to be amused or annoyed. Eventually the tension broke, and they laughed and giggled. I think each of them still believes he is my favorite.

Hard to think of parents having favorites, huh? I know it happens. Deion Sanders, the legendary football player, famously said that his favorite child is whichever one was the most recent to obey him. I like that approach!

But what about God? Does he have favorites? This question has puzzled theologians and believers for centuries. The Bible tells us that God loves all his children equally, yet there are stories where certain individuals receive special favor. Take David, for instance, described as a man after God's own heart. Or Joseph, who was given dreams and visions that set him apart from his brothers. Or even Job. He had a hedge of protection around him until God expressed his belief in his character and allowed the devil to destroy his life, not because he did anything wrong, but because his "uprightness" caused all hell to break loose in his life. Does this mean God had favorites, or is it that their actions and faith brought them closer to him in a unique way?

The concept of favor with God is complex. As parents we strive to love our children equally, yet we connect with them in different ways based on their personalities and our shared experiences. With God, his love is perfect and boundless, encompassing all his children.

When it comes to God's love for his children, he actually does play favorites. The only catch is every child of God is his favorite, and every child of God has his favor. Lisa Bevere once said, "God doesn't love us all the same; he loves each of us uniquely."[1] This echoes the sentiment of Saint Augustine, who said that God loves each of us as if there were only one of us.[2]

I had the opportunity to visit the beautiful country of Italy with my wife. It was the adventure of a lifetime. We were invited by our friends at Trinity Broadcasting Network to be part of a film with the great Italian tenor Andrea Bocelli. I had the privilege of traversing the Italian countryside on horseback with Andrea to talk about life, faith, and music.

During our journey on horseback, we rode into the small town of San Gimignano in Tuscany. Visiting this town, with its medieval architecture and rich history, felt like stepping back in time. When we arrived in the tenth-century cobblestone square, we beheld the Collegiata di Santa Maria Assunta, a church constructed in 1148—a simple but sacred treasure. The church, with its Romanesque architecture and serene ambiance, stood as a testament to the enduring faith and craftsmanship of the people who built it centuries ago.

We went inside and performed a few songs together. The acoustics of the church, designed to carry the sound of prayers and hymns, amplified our voices in a way that felt almost heavenly. When I looked up from inside the beautiful sanctuary, light was breaking through the circular stained glass above the altar. It was a fitting picture of how God's goodness, light, and favor blaze through each individual's life, like the sunlight shining through that stained-glass window.

Each pane of glass in a stained-glass window is unique— some blue, some red, some green—each with its own shape, design, and even imperfections. These panes reflect the diversity of our experiences: our joys and heartbreaks, our victories and losses. When light passes through, it illuminates each pane in a distinctive way, revealing the beauty and pur- pose in every piece. This interplay of light and color reminded me of how God's love and grace shine through our moments of pain, loss, and triumph, bringing out a beauty that could emerge only through these varied experiences.

Just as the light doesn't favor one pane over another but enhances each piece's design, God's love is vast and all-encompassing, and God, in his love, uses every experience we go through—both suffering and joy—to bring out his beauty in our lives. The stained glass becomes a powerful image of how our moments of brokenness and healing come together to reveal a grand mosaic of grace. Just as light shines through each imperfect pane, the joy of the Lord shines through our pain, using our struggles to display his goodness and mercy.

This experience in San Gimignano, with its rich history and spiritual depth, not only deepened my appreciation for Italy's cultural heritage but also expanded my understanding of divine love. Walking alongside Andrea, reflecting on life and faith and looking up at that illuminated stained glass, offered me a powerful insight into how God uses even our hardest moments to create a masterpiece of his light shining through us.

A FRAMEWORK FOR FAVOR

Favor, in the context of Christian theology, is often seen as an instrument of God's promise. It is a means through which God executes his divine will and purpose in the lives of believers. Favor is not merely a blessing but a tool for accomplishing God's greater plans.

It is common to mistakenly equate the by-products of favor—such as success, prosperity, or comfort—with favor itself. But favor is fundamentally about purpose rather than these material outcomes.

Favor serves a specific purpose in God's kingdom. It is designed to enable believers to fulfill their divine assignments and to bring glory to God. Therefore, favor is always aligned with God's ultimate plans and purposes for his people and his kingdom.

One of the profound truths about favor is its association with suffering. What people often perceive as favor, when viewed retrospectively, does not always feel like favor in the moment. This is because the favor of God frequently comes packaged with challenges and hardships. It's important to understand that while God allows us to go through difficult times, he does so for our growth and development—not to harm us. God promises never to harm his children, but this does not mean they will not experience pain. Rather, in his wisdom and goodness, God repurposes pain as productive and necessary for the growth and maturity of the believer. These challenges refine us, build our characters, and prepare us for the purposes he has set for our lives.

While the Scripture does not always explain how to gain favor, it does provide guidance on how it can be lost. "God opposes the proud but gives grace to the humble" (James 4:6 NLT). Those who exalt themselves will be brought low (Matthew 23:12). These verses emphasize the importance of humility in maintaining God's favor.

The favor of God is both unexplainable and unmerited. It represents preferential treatment that cannot be earned by human efforts but was earned by Jesus and bestowed upon believers through grace. Favor is thus a divine gift that reflects God's grace and sovereignty.

Favor is a function of grace in a believer's life, meant to accomplish specific purposes for God's kingdom and glory. It is through grace that believers receive favor, empowering them to fulfill God's plans and manifest his will on earth. Favor is a complex and multifaceted concept in Christian theology. It is not simply about experiencing blessings or avoiding hardships but is intrinsically linked to purpose, growth, and God's sovereign plans. Understanding favor requires recognizing its association with suffering, the importance of humility, and that its foundation is grace and joy.

BOMBS AWAY: DETONATE THE JOY BOMB

From the very start, we acknowledged a tough truth: Your joy is under attack. In this book I wanted to put at your fingertips the codes for detonating the joy of Jesus in your life.

Life isn't neutral; it's constantly throwing challenges, disappointments, and losses our way. But as we've journeyed through each of the Beatitudes, these "codes" to a blessed life, we've discovered that joy doesn't have to be fragile. Jesus's teachings flip our expectations upside down, showing us that real joy—the kind that lasts—isn't about escaping hardship but about finding God's strength in the middle of it. With every beatitude, Jesus opened a new pathway to a joy that doesn't fade but grows stronger with every obstacle we overcome. Each one peels back a layer of God's character and invites us to live out a joy that not only fills us but spills over to the world around us.

Each beatitude is a new layer, showing us the very heart of God for his people. The Beatitudes reveal not just his power but his overwhelming love and grace. Imagine a God so good that in every hardship or persecution he meets us with a promise of comfort, hope, and joy. In our deepest sorrows, when we feel most abandoned, God is there, ready to lift, heal, and restore us.

And what's amazing is how the Beatitudes lead us to reflect more and more of God's own nature. In the eyes of the world, characteristics such as meekness or peace might seem weak, but in God's eyes they are strengths. Meekness is not weakness; it's strength under control. Peace is not passivity; it's the courage to pursue harmony in a divided world. When we embody these traits, we become more like him, growing closer to the image of Christ with every step. This transformation is ongoing—a journey of becoming more like God each day. And though we won't fully arrive this side of heaven, the Beatitudes give us a glimpse of the wholeness we will experience in eternity.

Let's walk through each of these codes once more and see how, together, they invite us to a joy-filled, transformed life.

CODE ONE: JOY IN SPIRITUAL POVERTY

We began with the idea of being "poor in spirit." This is a counterintuitive starting place because we're taught that happiness is about having more—more success, more confidence, more control. But Jesus said the opposite: "Blessed are the poor in spirit." Spiritual poverty means recognizing our need for God, understanding that we can't do it all on our own. When we come to him empty-handed, he fills us with a joy that can't be bought or earned. The beauty here is that joy is found not in self-sufficiency but in surrender.

When we come to the end of ourselves, it's not the end of our stories—it's often just the beginning. In this humility we discover that joy isn't about how much we can achieve but about the fullness we find when we open our hands and say, "God, I need you." Our culture often tells us that strength is in independence, but the Beatitudes flip that on its head. The joy that comes from spiritual poverty isn't something we find by building ourselves up; it's what we receive when we're willing to be built up by God himself.

CODE TWO: JOY IN MOURNING

The next beatitude takes us even deeper: "Blessed are those who mourn." Here Jesus tells us that there's joy in vulnerability. Mourning isn't just about sadness; it's about letting ourselves feel deeply, being honest with our pain, and trusting God with it. When we mourn, we open our hearts to God's comfort.

Consider this: We live in a world that says, "Toughen up. Don't let them see you cry." But Jesus says the opposite. He invites us to bring our pain to him, to let ourselves be real about the hurts we carry. In this space of honesty, God meets us with his comfort, and this comfort is unlike anything the world can offer. The joy here is a healing joy. It's the peace that enters in after a storm, a balm to a wounded heart that doesn't deny the pain but overcomes it with love.

Joy in mourning seems like a paradox, but it's a reminder that God isn't afraid of our brokenness. In fact, he meets us most powerfully there. This beatitude shows us that joy isn't the absence of hardship; it's the presence of God with us through it.

CODE THREE: JOY IN HUMILITY

Then Jesus said, "Blessed are the meek." In a world that prizes control and ambition, humility can feel like weakness. But in God's economy, humility is strength. Meekness isn't about being passive; it's about living with a heart surrendered to God's authority.

When we let go of the need to prove ourselves, we find joy in a freedom that the world can't offer. Humility allows us to receive God's strength, to rely on his power instead of our own, and that reliance brings joy. In humility we discover that God is the one who lifts us up, who promotes and elevates us in ways we can't achieve on our own.

Think about this: When we're humble, we stop striving for recognition or fighting for control. We're free to experience God's provision because we're not chasing after things to prove our worth. This beatitude reminds us that joy comes not from being the biggest or the best but from knowing we're fully accepted by God. This freedom allows us to live in the moment, to trust God's timing, and to find joy in the journey instead of constantly striving for the next accomplishment.

CODE FOUR: JOY IN SPIRITUAL HUNGER

"Blessed are those who hunger and thirst for righteousness." Hunger is uncomfortable. Thirst is demanding. But Jesus promises that when we crave God's righteousness—his ways, his justice, his heart—we will be filled. The world offers us plenty of "snacks" to fill the void, but they only leave us hungry again.

True joy comes from a life centered on God, a life that seeks him above all else. When we direct our desires toward him, we find a satisfaction that is deep and lasting. This hunger for righteousness draws us closer to God and fills us with a joy that depends not on circumstances but on the fullness of his presence in our lives.

Imagine craving not just food but the presence of God in your life. This is the joy that goes beyond surface happiness; it's the fulfillment that comes from knowing our desires are aligned with his purposes. When our hearts beat in sync with God's heart, we experience a joy that is steady, deep, and unwavering.

CODE FIVE: JOY IN FORGIVENESS

"Blessed are the merciful." In a culture that often tells us to hold grudges and get even, forgiveness is radical. But Jesus calls us to show mercy because it's the path to freedom—for ourselves and for others. Forgiveness breaks the chains of bitterness and resentment, allowing us to live in the joy of a heart unburdened.

Mercy isn't easy. It goes against our natural instincts to protect ourselves, keep score, make people pay for their mistakes. But Jesus shows us that joy flows when we let go, when we release the need for revenge or bitterness. In mercy we reflect God's heart, opening the way for joy to enter in. This joy is a powerful kind of freedom, one that liberates us from past hurts and allows us to move forward with open hearts.

Forgiveness might seem like a gift we give others, but it's a gift we give ourselves too. It's a decision to stop letting our pasts rob us of joy in the present. Through mercy we're able to let go of the burden and embrace a joy that flows freely, unhindered by grudges or bitterness.

CODE SIX: JOY IN PURITY OF HEART

"Blessed are the pure in heart, for they will see God." Purity of heart is about clarity of purpose, alignment of our intentions with God's will. It's not about moral perfection but about living with a single-minded focus on God's love and his way.

When our hearts are pure, we see God at work more clearly. We're no longer distracted by mixed motives or hidden agendas. Joy flows from knowing that we are aligned with God's will, that we're seeing him in our lives, our relationships, our everyday moments. Purity is an invitation to deeper intimacy with God, and that intimacy brings profound joy.

With a pure heart, we're able to see the world differently. We see God's fingerprints in places we might have missed before. Purity doesn't mean living without mistakes; it means living with intentionality, with a heart that's devoted to seeking God first. In this state of openness and honesty, we encounter a joy that's undiluted, a joy that's both simple and profound, because it comes from seeing God's presence all around us.

CODE SEVEN: JOY IN PEACEMAKING

"Blessed are the peacemakers." Peacemaking isn't about avoiding conflict; it's about stepping into it with a heart set on reconciliation. Jesus calls us to bring peace in a world full of division, to be active participants in building harmony where others sow discord.

Peacemaking takes courage, and it's rooted in a joy that goes beyond personal comfort—it's a joy that comes from knowing we're reflecting God's heart. When we act as peacemakers, we're living out our identity as God's children, and that brings a joy that is strong and steady, a joy that lasts even in the face of opposition.

This kind of joy isn't passive. It's an active force, an intentional choice to bridge divides, forgive, and bring unity. The joy of peacemaking comes from knowing that we're agents of God's love, that we're part of his mission to heal and restore. When we work for peace, we find joy in seeing relationships mended, communities strengthened, and God's presence felt in our midst.

CODE EIGHT: JOY IN PERSECUTION

Finally, Jesus told us, "Blessed are those who are persecuted because of righteousness." This is perhaps the hardest to grasp, but it's also one of the most powerful. When we face hardship for living out God's truth, we're aligning with Jesus himself. The world may push back, but we're grounded in a joy that's rooted in the eternal.

Persecution reminds us that we're part of a kingdom that is not of this world, that our lives have a purpose beyond ourselves. This joy isn't about avoiding difficulty but about knowing that every hardship brings us closer to the heart of God and to the hope of future glory. When we endure persecution for his sake, we're participating in something larger than ourselves, part of a legacy of believers who have found joy in suffering for Christ.

SET IT OFF!

This is it! This is where the fuse meets the spark. After every truth we've dug into, every moment we've shared, we're finally here—to let the joy bomb go off. Jesus didn't give us the Beatitudes as some lofty ideals to chase; he gave us a radical road map to resilient, unbreakable joy. The kind of joy that doesn't shrink back or fade away—the kind that lives deep, grows richer with time, and lights up everything around it.

Imagine what it feels like to live from this kind of joy. It's more than a quick lift or a good mood. It's a steady, rooted joy that fills every corner of our lives, spilling into even the smallest moments. It's that sense of peace when everything else is uncertain, that confidence in knowing that we're walking in step with something bigger than ourselves, that hope in the darkest times that somehow, someway, there's more ahead. This joy doesn't just uplift—it changes us, and, through us, it changes others.

The Beatitudes have shown us a way of life in which God's joy flows freely, meeting us exactly where we are. This joy is born from letting go of the need to keep up, from daring to face grief with honesty, from allowing ourselves to depend on God even when we feel empty. It grows through the freedom of forgiveness, the quiet strength of humility, the pull toward justice, and the peace we bring to others. And yes, even when things get uncomfortable or unpopular, this joy stays unshaken. Each step, each code, has brought us to this place.

So now take a moment to picture what happens when you let this joy bomb go off. Imagine a life in which joy fills every part of you and overflows—a joy so real that it lights up your family, friendships, and community. Picture the kind of presence you carry when you bring peace where there was tension, when you bring hope into hard places, when you show love that can't help but break down walls. This is the power of a life lit up by God's joy.

This joy isn't just for you; it's meant to overflow, to reach the people around you, to plant seeds of hope and healing in lives that need it. When you carry this kind of joy, you're a reminder of God's goodness, his peace, and his promises. You become a spark in a world hungry for something real.

So breathe it in, let it settle deep, and then—*set it off*. Live in the joy that Jesus has given you. Let it change you, strengthen you, and transform everything you touch. This is the joy-bomb way of life—a life full, rooted in God's presence, ready to make a difference. Embrace it, carry it, and watch as God's joy does what only his joy can do: change everything.

Set it off.

NOTES

INTRODUCTION

1. John Piper, host, *Messages by Desiring God*, podcast, "Let Your Passion Be Single," Desiring God, November 12, 1999, https://www.desiringgod.org/messages/let -your-passion-be-single.
2. As cited in "Is Happiness Different from Joy?" interview with Randy Alcorn, *Ask Pastor John* podcast, episode 734, November 23, 2015, Desiring God, https://www.desiringgod.org/interviews/is -happiness-different-from-joy.
3. Alcorn, interview, "Is Happiness Different from Joy?"
4. Alcorn, interview, "Is Happiness Different from Joy?"
5. Alcorn, interview, "Is Happiness Different from Joy?" See also James K. A. Smith, *Desiring the Kingdom: Worship, Worldview, and Cultural Formation* (Baker Academic, 2009).
6. Alcorn, interview, "Is Happiness Different from Joy?"
7. Alcorn, interview, "Is Happiness Different from Joy?" citing C. S. Lewis, *Mere Christianity* (HarperOne, 1952).

CODE ONE: HAPPY ARE THE SPIRITUALLY BANKRUPT

1. Based on Lyubomirsky's research on behalf of ConAgra's Reddi-wip. See Steven Macdonald, "7 Feel-Good Examples of 'Joy Marketing' Campaigns," Hubspot Marketing, December 15, 2015, updated August 25 2017, https://blog.hubspot.com/marketing/joy-marketing -campaigns.
2. Oswald Chambers, *My Utmost for His Highest*, updated ed., ed. James Reimann (Discovery House, 1992), July 21.
3. David Scott, "Family Plan: Shaq Reveals How His Children Don't Get Equal Treatment as NBA Legend Says 'We Ain't Rich, I'm Rich,'" *The U.S. Sun*, September 20, 2024, https://www.the-sun.com/sport/12503296 /nba-shaq-children-wealthy-treatment/.

CODE TWO: HAPPY ARE THE DESPERATELY SAD

1. David P. Gushee and Glen H. Stassen, *Kingdom Ethics: Following Jesus in Contemporary Context* (InterVarsity Press, 2003), 59.
2. Chip Dodd, *The Voice of the Heart: A Call to Full Living* (Sage Hill, 2014).
3. Mary Page James and Dan Witters, "Daily Loneliness Afflicts One in Five in U.S.," Gallup, October 15, 2024, news.gallup.com/poll/651881/daily-loneliness-afflicts -one-five.aspx.
4. Jim C. Collins and Jerry I. Porras, *Built to Last: Successful Habits of Visionary Companies* (HarperBusiness, 2002), 44.

CODE THREE: HAPPY ARE THE INTENTIONALLY HUMBLE

1. Muhammad Ali Center, "Meet Ali: In His Own Words," https://alicenter.org/meet-ali/in-his-own-words/.
2. "Cristiano Ronaldo: I Am Better Than Lionel Messi," BBC News, Nov 5, 2015, https://www.bbc.com/sport/av/football/34739443.
3. Lauren Moraski, "Kanye West: 'I Am Picasso' and 'Steve Jobs,'" CBS News, February 27, 2013, https://www.cbsnews.com/news/kanye-west-i-am-picasso-and-steve-jobs/.
4. Tony Evans, *Kingdom Man: Every Man's Destiny, Every Woman's Dream* (Tyndale House, 2012), 38.
5. Erwin McManus and Aaron McManus, *Mind Shift*, podcast, "The Elegance of Soft Power," episode 31, March 22, 2024.
6. McManus and McManus, "The Elegance of Soft Power."
7. McManus and McManus, "The Elegance of Soft Power."

CODE FOUR: HAPPY ARE THE INSATIABLY HUNGRY

1. James Clear, *Atomic Habits: An Easy and Proven Way to Build Good Habits and Break Bad Ones* (Avery, 2018), 47–50.
2. Clear, *Atomic Habits*, 48.
3. Clear, *Atomic Habits*, 47–50.
4. Peter Greer and Greg Lafferty, *40/40 Vision: Clarifying Your Mission in Midlife* (InterVarsity Press, 2015), 35.
5. Greer and Lafferty, *40/40 Vision*, 50.
6. C. S. Lewis, *Mere Christianity* (HarperOne, 1952), 121.

CODE SIX: HAPPY ARE THE PASSIONATELY PURE

1. John Piper, "God Is Most Glorified in Us When We Are Most Satisfied in Him," sermon, Desiring God, October 13, 2012, https://www.desiringgod.org/messages/god-is-most-glorified-in-us-when-we-are-most-satisfied-in-him.

CODE EIGHT: HAPPY ARE THE WILLINGLY PERSECUTED

1. Lisa Bevere, "Lisa Bevere: God Does Not Love Us Equally (James Robison / LIFE Today)," lifetodaytv, YouTube channel, posted October 3, 2014, https://www.youtube.com/watch?v=zueWvszzWPY.
2. Augustine, *Confessions*, 3.11.

From the Publisher

GREAT BOOKS

ARE EVEN BETTER WHEN THEY'RE SHARED!

Help other readers find this one:

- Post a review at your favorite online bookseller

- Post a picture on a social media account and share why you enjoyed it

- Send a note to a friend who would also love it—or better yet, give them a copy

Thanks for reading!